Life Code-
The Vedic Code Book

An In-depth View of the AKASHIC Records of
Your Past, Present and Future

Swami Ram Charran

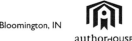

Bloomington, IN   Milton Keynes, UK

authorHOUSE®

AuthorHouse™
1663 Liberty Drive, Suite 200
Bloomington, IN 47403
www.authorhouse.com
Phone: 1-800-839-8640

AuthorHouse™ UK Ltd.
500 Avebury Boulevard
Central Milton Keynes, MK9 2BE
www.authorhouse.co.uk
Phone: 08001974150

First published by AuthorHouse 3/22/2007

ISBN: 1-4259-4898-7 (sc)
ISBN: 978-1-4259-9943-8 (dj)

Library of Congress Control Number: 2006908034

Printed in the United States of America
Bloomington, Indiana

This book is printed on acid-free paper.

To my children – Luana, Leukas & Luresa

The Ripples

My grandfather took me for a walk one day when I was about seven and stopped by a fishing pond. "Please sit down," he invited, patting the ground next to him. "Now find a small stone, please," he instructed.

"What?"

"A stone. Please find a small stone and throw it into the pond."

Searching around me, I grabbed a pebble and threw it as far as I could.

"Tell me what you see," he requested.

Straining my eyes to not miss a single detail, I looked at the water's surface. "I see ripples, Grandpa."

"Where did the ripples come from, son?"

"From the pebble I threw into the pond."

"Please reach your hand into the water and stop the ripples," he instructed me.

Not understanding, I stuck my hand into the water as a ripple neared, only to cause more ripples. I now was completely baffled. *Where was this lesson going? Why was Grandpa asking me to do this?* I wondered. Puzzled, I looked at him.

"Were you able to stop the ripples with your hand, my child?" he asked.

"No, of course not." I was beginning to feel a little uncomfortable.

"Could you have stopped the ripples then?"

"No, in fact, I only caused more ripples."

"What if you had stopped the pebble from entering the water to begin with?" Grandpa smiled such a beautiful smile; I just could not be upset.

"Next time you are unhappy with your life, catch the 'stone' before it hits the water. Do not spend time trying to undo what you have done. Rather, change what you are going to do before you do it." Grandpa looked at me with such love in his eyes.

"But tell me how will I know what I am going to do before I do it?"

"Take the responsibility for living your own life, my son. See, your actions will create lots of splashes in your life, but remember that the waves that come from those splashes have a knock-on effect on all of your fellow creatures," he explained.

"Remember that you are responsible for what you put into your circle as that circle will touch many other circles, too. You will need to live in a way that allows the good that comes from your circle to send the peace of that goodness to others. The splash that comes from anger or jealousy will send those feelings to other circles. You are responsible for both."

Aaah, I think I understood! I realized that each person creates the inner peace or discord that flows out into the world. We cannot create world peace if we ourselves are riddled with inner conflict, hatred, doubt or anger. Whatever is splashing around inside of us is spilling out into the world, creating beauty or discord with all other circles of life. We radiate the feelings and thoughts that we hold inside, whether we speak them or not. So, ultimately it is all up to us!

This reminded me of the eternal wisdom: *Your life is not a coincidence. It is merely a reflection of you!*

–Author unknown

Duty is God. Work is worship.

Preface

After pondering the sad and tormented state of the world and after undertaking considerable research, I decided to write a series of books that would help people live completely happy and satisfied lives. I hope that with the knowledge contained in this book you will achieve a better understanding of yourself and your relationship to God and His Universe.

God is always here for us as a force of goodness. We create our own future karma, bad or good, through our actions and reactions. Everyone chooses to follow a path of prosperity or a path of destruction. Religion was not made by God, but by mankind. We all contain Godliness within ourselves.

Each of us has an exact replica of the 108 elements contained in the Universe; therefore, each of us is an exact image of the Universe. If we stop breathing, we will die shortly thereafter, thus the air we breathe can be considered divine, because it is necessary for life, just as God is.

This train of thought enables us to call light energy a divine source. Just as important as light and air are, we should also consider knowledge, water, Earth, Sun, and Moon equally important, for without them we humans would cease to exist. All of these elements are contained in the human body, making it an ideal temple of God.

If you need to change your life, the Universe would also have to change with you. Do you realize that every time a child is born, the Universe must rearrange itself to match the new entrance into the world? Have you ever thought about the fact that each time a child is conceived from a few minutes of lovemaking, the subsequent events create tremendous changes?

For example, let us say that it takes five minutes to conceive a child, followed by nine months of gestation, then minutes or hours of labor and all the attendant services –

doctors, nurses, hospitals, pharmacies, baby food companies, clothing manufacturers, diaper services, and so on. As the child grows, other connections, such as schools, teachers, friends, toy companies, and so on experience the change that started with the few minutes leading to conception.

Can you now understand the effect that each human action has on the entire Universe? Needless to say, if a child becomes a doctor, lawyer, scientist, president or terrorist, imagine the effect of that birth on the world.

Each of us should realize that what we eat, drink or wear has a tremendous influence on the way we respond to the Universe and the way the Universe responds to us. For example, if we always wear black clothes, we restrict the effects of light on the body (black absorbs light), thus causing a shortage of Vitamin D, which is necessary for our circulation and thought processes. A shortage of this vitamin can affect the way we function and so create negative effects.

In addition, as babies, we drank milk, which contains the same proteins found in the human body and in red meat. Therefore, if we eat red meat, we are technically asking our bodies to digest themselves. This is detrimental to our health. Red meat contains *urea*, which slows down the *synapses* of the nervous system, thereby causing sluggishness. A slowing down of human response means loss of opportunities and an increase in depression, employment problems, irregular behavior and so on. That leads to further problems and eventually suffering and poverty.

In conclusion, with proper knowledge about ourselves, the Universe, the avoidance of wearing black clothes exclusively, the abstinence of eating red meat and the awareness of our surroundings through spiritual connections, we can safely say that human beings are all capable of enjoying life to the fullest.

This book is designed to impart that knowledge and set you on your way to a richer, happier life.

Contents

Acknowledgements &
A Message from the Author

This book probes a complex system through which logical and rational conclusions can be made concerning your purpose in this life and why you experience any and all things as you make the journey from birth to death and beyond. There is no longer any doubt that people in the world today are seeking solutions and answers as to why the world is experiencing so much distress and destruction. People are in awe of tsunamis, hurricanes, earthquakes, terrorism, tornadoes and their immensity at this time in history. Many individuals are worried about the existence of God and whether God is truly a force that can help them in the wake of these scary events taking place in the world.

The Aryan Culture of Celestial Correspondences, which we call the Vedic Code of Science as revealed by the ancient sages, is an excellent tool to open doors to the future and provide the ultimate answers to all the questions that every individual or collective group may have. Unlike astrology or psychic guessing, reasonably intelligent people can understand the Vedic Code and, like mathematics, it works whenever it is applied and not when a superstitious application or interpretation is made.

Hopefully in the next century, the Vedic Code, as presented in this book, will provide the most dramatic evidence that the trend of the world or of any individual can be anticipated in a direct way, so as to avoid disappointments and failure in life. No longer will there be a sense of insecurity and insignificance. People will be able to directly tell when something will happen in their life through the secrets of the Vedic Code of Science.

I would like to thank several authors, who have contributed their knowledge and inspired me to connect the Vedic Code of Science to modern mathematics and physics. Firstly, I greatly appreciate the inspiration I received from reading Gary Zukav's book, *The Wuli Masters*, and especially the book written by Mr. Joseph F. Goodavage, *The Space Age Science*. I would also like to extend special thanks to my great gurus and teachers of ancient Vedic sciences, who have inspired me with this great knowledge that I have been able to use to help thousands of people who were lost. Several organizations, such as AFA and others whom I have mentioned at the back of this book, have contributed tremendous information on events to prove that the Vedic Code of Science is a genuine system for successful and prosperous living.

Having become a Swami (Wisdom Master) in the course of my service to help others, my studies have led me to believe that the Universe is a living Universe in the shape of man, and that the Universe has an order just as Einstein concluded. The Vedic Code circumvents the universal order in all the ages, because it magnificently reflects all the laws of nature. It is the greatest body of knowledge a human being can possess, bar none.

Timing is the all-important element for everything one undertakes. The simple facts of nature have been recognized by the greatest minds of all ages, including the seers, who wrote the Bible:

> All things have their season, and in their
> time all things pass under Heaven. A
> time to be born and a time to die. A time
> to plant and a time to pluck up that
> which is planted. A time to kill, and a time
> to heal. A time to destroy, and a time to
> build. A time to weep, and a time to laugh...
> *Ecclesiastes: 3: 1-8*

These are pure philosophical codes. The Bible is full of them.

Nothing can happen until the time is right for it to happen. When you observe this over a long period, it will not make you fatalistic, as some think. Knowing the right and wrong times to act – *in advance* – gives you an enormous advantage. The Vedic Code can broaden your choice. It is like having tomorrow's newspaper today. It gives you a tremendous edge.

Long ago certain wise saints and sages kept secret their knowledge of the Universe so that they could use it for themselves. After developing the Vedic Code of Science, they selfishly hid their knowledge in symbolism so that they could use their power to guide others without exposing their secrets. They passed their secret knowledge only to their initiates or disciples.

Space age science, however, is now throwing a clear light of objective reasoning into new areas of human knowledge. As a result of the development of computer sciences, we are now able to interpret information at a higher speed and thus expand our levels of observance and circle of vision in life.

The fact is that if powerful forces from the surrounding Universe have an effect on human life and, if these forces can be measured using proven mathematical calculations, then a number or a code can indicate when certain events like marriage, accidents or birth take place accurately. If all individuals can use such a system, then not only will we have a more peaceful life but also life on Earth will be more enjoyable and the world will be a safer place in which to live.

As a Swami, I have successfully guided thousands of individuals in their lives over the last 20 years. I have also used the Vedic Code of Science to predict many natural disasters in the world, such as the World Trade Center destruction, the earthquakes in California, hurricanes in Florida, and others many months before they happened.

Please note that knowledge is a two-edged sword; it can be used to create as well as destroy. I hope the readers of this book will use the knowledge presented by the Vedic Code of Science only for good purposes and for the progress of the world and mankind.

With great love and respect, I welcome all of you to the Vedic Code of Science.

How to Read This Book

The first thing you need to know before being able to use this book for your life guidance and benefit is your birthdate. With the help of your birthdate, you find your Vedic Birth Code in Chapter 6 on Table 6:1.

With your Vedic Birth Code, you will find most of the things about yourself, such as your Childbirth Code, which tells you about the codes that you inherited from your parents and ancestral line, your Hereditary Code, Meditation Code, Fertility Code, and others. The information in these codes is based solely on your Vedic Birth Code.

Additional information about your life, as found in your Life Code, which tells you about your path in life, your Sexual, Love and Marriage Codes, as well as some others, combines with your Vedic Birth Code to determine additional Vedic Codes for interpretation.

In the chapters on the Vedic Location Code, Career Code and Disaster Code, some of them are independently interpreted and are combined with your Vedic Birth Code to give further enlightenment about your life. As you may observe, the Vedic Birth Code is used constantly in all of the chapters, so make sure you determine that code first.

Because I am unable to cover all of the Vedic Codes in one book, I have attached in Appendix 1 a list of additional Vedic Codes that I will discuss in Volume 2, an upcoming publication.

I have provided some Vedic Codes and birthdates of famous people and important events in Appendix 2 and 3, which you may use to experiment with the Vedic Code of Science system to see if you can do your own forecasting and predictions as they relate to these famous people. You may also understand better why they have acted a certain way.

I hope you find this book beneficial in answering some questions about yourself. If any questions remain unanswered, however, please feel free to call the Heendu Learning Center, Inc., in Miami, Florida – 305-253-5410.

With great love and respect, I welcome you to the Vedic Code of Science.

Swami Ramcharran

Introduction

Each person is unique. Everyone has a different set of fingerprints. Everyone, who has died, had unique fingerprints, just as those yet to be born will have unique fingerprints. Even identical twins do not have the same fingerprints. Law enforcement agencies have proven these statements to be true. How is it possible that each person has his or her own unique fingerprints as well as unique voiceprints? These unique characteristics make each of us different from the other and show that we are unique human beings, each of us being a special person in this world.

Do you realize that at the time of your birth, a unique moment was created in the Universe in terms of the arrangement of the planets at that exact time, a period that can never again be duplicated? Each of these moments can be identified by such factors as:

☐ Where were the planets at the exact moment you took your first breath?
☐ Where were your father or other family members at that critical moment?
☐ What was the condition of the political world at that moment?
☐ Where was the Sun or Moon at the moment when your life began?
☐ Who was the president then?

And so on...

That moment, marked by these and other factors, can never be repeated again. So, together all forces of the Universe created unique fingerprints for you. At your birth, a timeline, which started approximately nine months earlier, was given kinetic energy to grow and move forward, and it continues until you die. A timeline must have a beginning, middle, and end. This book is concerned with the middle range of the timeline, what takes place between the time you took your first breath and when you will take your last.

As you read this book, you are blessed to include in your timeline the knowledge of who you are, where you came from, what your purpose is and where you are headed in this life. This knowledge will enable you to assess your life in a manner that is unique to your fingerprint.

You will learn about your place in the Universe and how to harmonize with it in such a way that you can experience great prosperity, happiness and success in life, even though you thought your life would always be miserable. You will learn about your strengths and weaknesses, how to take advantage of them and how to make them work for you to achieve the greatest luxury of all – peace of mind.

In this book, you will learn why you have the type of family you have, why you have your particular marriage partner, why you have the children you have, and why children behave in a certain way. You will also learn whether you are living in the right home, the right country, the right city, town or village and whether you have the right job or not.

Many times, we wonder why we have accidents, disappointments, sickness, quarrels, fights, disease, imprisonment, trials, divorces, financial problems, and more. In this book, you should find the answers to all of your questions.

Chapter 1

Introduction to the
Vedic Code of Science

Since the beginning of their civilizations, the ancient Aryans and Atlanteans had the play of the Universe and believed that basic forces make the Universe work in a precise and orderly manner. Albert Einstein was indeed correct when he said, "God does not play dice with the world." The ancient scientists developed a system that would be fully integrated with earthly life.

They called their system the Akashic Code of Records. Through this system, their scientific advances developed hand in hand, springing from the certainty that in the ebb and flow of the Universe, all is one that is encased in this unique system of universal laws. Life does not end with death or the function of the Moon with dawn. The movement of a dog's ears is not an event without effect, just as the appearance of a star at a child's birth not an occurrence without meaning.

The Vedic Code of Science, unlike Western science, uses the method of predictive cycles based on birth and death, circular motion of time and the thousands of natural cycles in the Universe. The ancient Aryans and Atlanteans were keen observers of the cycles of nature and, as such, decided to record these observances in the form of symbolism. These scientists were able to determine that there is a set of constant values that form the basic measurement of all life in the Universe. These values became the base system of the Hindu science called Vedic mathematics.

The numbers from 0 to 9 determine all the forces in the Universe, for when we add the coordinates of our birth, the end value equals one of the numbers between 0 and 9. Vedic Mathematics, designed as a divine science, helped the Aryans understand the very heartbeat of the Universe, the actual function of every being on Earth and the Universe and, last but not least, the system that would help mankind experience the most bliss, prosperity and happiness while alive on Earth. The key to all of this, of course, is knowledge.

Even today in our society, the person with the most knowledge generally fares better in life. However, the knowledge that I refer to is beyond that. It is so deep that it guides you towards happiness every moment of the hour, the day, the month and even the year. This knowledge tells you when you are veering into the wrong, as opposed to the right, boundaries in specific situations. This knowledge lets you know if your partner is happy or unhappy with you, in addition to letting you know if you will be wealthy or poor, why something unfortunate happened and how to correct it.

Wouldn't it be interesting to know exactly what will happen if your mother or father ended up in the ICU in the hospital? Instead of sitting for hours in uncertainty, crying or wondering if he or she was going to die, wouldn't it be more comforting if you knew that the operation would be successful? Or that it would be worthwhile to remove that person to another location for better treatment where they can actually be saved instead of letting him or her succumb to death? Not the least, would it not be interesting if you knew how long your job would last or which year would bring your business more success or less profit? Or whether you are going to have a son or daughter with your spouse? Would it not be great to know which foods are healthier for your diet, why you have acid stomach, cancer or other diseases or why you are not able to conceive children, and more?

This book will hopefully afford you this knowledge to a certain extent. It is very difficult to place all that I have been fortunate to learn into one book and, thus, I hope to achieve that in several books. It is understandable that the kind of knowledge and insight I present in these pages might be used in a negative way, too. I hope, however, that through this knowledge, people may realize that every bad action leads to more bad experiences and that every good action leads to many returned benefits. Every experience or event can be explained in life, if one lives a truthful life. Newton's law of action and reaction never fails and is therefore the basic law of the Universe that governs our existence on Earth.

In practicality, the ancient Aryans wished to illustrate that if something exists in reality it must have a counterpart that is an opposite. Also, if something has a birth it must have a death and, last but not least, if something has a body, it must have a soul, and so on. The ancient Vedic Code of Science used the movement of the planets as a timepiece to assess when certain events would occur between the coordinates of life and death. Similarly we use the clock (which is based on the Sun) to time our schedule between the beginning of the day and the night. These scientists have provided formulae to calculate the points of major importance that occur between the beginning (of anything) and the end (of anything). The birth and death of the soul (and the body) plays an important part in the calculation of these events.

Action results in reaction (karma), which determines the path of that person or entity as it strives to achieve a parallel flow with the Universe.

If people are made aware that this Vedic Code of Science exists as a wonderful guide, they will plan for a better and more prosperous life. They will realize that the natural law of action and reaction is an equation that applies not only to science but also to every facet of nature. If the Vedic Code of Science gains its true recognition in the world, then mankind can be guided to properly follow the natural laws of the Universe. We need to let the world know that the Vedic Code of Science – not simply astrology – is really an advanced science of life. I am depending on the Western scientists to provide the proper response and guidance to people, who seek their advice on this Vedic Code system.

The Vedic Code system of the ancient Aryans is differentiated from Western systems by the presupposition of the universal cycles of birth, sleep and renewal and by the fact that death and renewal are addressed as causalities far more serious and meaningful than they are considered in the West. Thus, in the Vedic Code of Science, the appearance of troubled situations is not only coincidental with fluctuation in financial income; it is in fact the cause of those fluctuations. And the incestuous abuse of a child may be not only an event that took place independently, but also may be rooted in the long line of family ancestry. Similarly, the genetic code of the parents may pass not only their physical characteristics on to the child, but also their spiritual characteristics.

An example would be a subliminal code that transfers karmic debts of actions from the ancestors before that. Think of it this way: If a pregnant woman is physically abused during her pregnancy, all resultant emotions are transferred to the child she is carrying. Compare that to a pregnant woman, who is showered with love, music, romance and affection. This explains why criminal behavioral characteristics often appear in children with fathers, who committed crimes in their earlier life. I have personally witnessed over 27,000 cases like this. In addition to this, the Vedic Code system contains a cure for this kind of "heredity" and can be used to avoid emotional disasters by applying certain scientific remedies recommended by the Vedic Code of Science to one's life.

In this respect, the Vedic Code of Science is much more simple and direct than the Western system. The simplicity is such that almost anyone on Earth can learn the basic rules to follow for successful and prosperous living. I have helped many families, who were surprised

4

when their four-year-old kids grasped some of the basic formulae quickly. In this simple system, you do not need to understand the complex science behind the forces that control you; you need only to apply them to your life. This is where the "key code" system I have developed will make you see quickly how easy it is to comprehend the code and apply it to others around you, too; thereby explaining their behaviors in addition to yours.

Each Person is Unique

Law enforcement agencies have proved many times over that everyone is unique in this world because each one has a different fingerprint. Because time moves forward and no one can stop time or change the flow of time; all things in the Universe are given a value at each moment of time. Each moment of time is different from every other moment of time. A person can never be born in the same place and at the tame time as another person. This is what makes each one of us unique. Therefore, your time and place of birth are called 'unique coordinates' in the graphic analysis of universal time.

Each month, each day and each year is different from each other, and so your month of birth, your day of birth, your hour of birth and your birth location are unique values that represent only you and no one else in this Universe.

The Basic System of the Vedic Code of Science

In this elaborate system and, of course, in the Vedic Codes, the prime force to contend with is not the solar system, the stars or the planets but indeed the Sun as the "male" principal and the Moon as the "female" principal – and the connection between these two. As they meet the third force, which is the Earth, they form a powerful triangle of resultant forces. In the form of electrons and protons, these resultant forces are all rearranged constantly to match the experiences of each person individually. We in turn form a special coordinate at every action at every moment. As humans, creatures and plants, we affect each other tremendously. The actions of others affect us as we affect the others.

Research of events and occurrences was conducted on over 27,000 individuals from various parts of the world and recorded as part of this effort. I hope this work will be beneficial to the scientific community at large.

Ancient scientists determined that the Sun in our solar system determines our daily activities and perceptions, so the day assigned to our birth is very important. The Moon determines our birth of month and so the movement of the Moon and the Sun together constitutes our birth coordinates in the Universe. These two heavenly bodies control the tides, the weather, the seasons, the way we live, the way we work, the way we eat and so on.

Life depends on crops and the crops in turn depend on the configurations of the heavenly bodies. Thus, agricultural calculations are particularly complete, and differentiation is made between planting seeds and planting seedlings from which flowers and fruits will grow. But social and cultural events, too, are plotted out – weddings, housewarmings, entertainment premiers, plays, ballets and more.

Lifeline vs. Timeline

Usually, the business of predicting the future belongs to astrologers, psychics and science fiction writers. Most of these groups preach strongly that our complete life is predetermined, and that there is a blueprint of our destiny written in the stars and so on. This may be true to an extent, as far as these groups are concerned. However, I believe that it can be proven that nobody's future is predetermined, but rather is created by their own actions within a set range of experiences. Our future can only be one of two containment factors – negative or positive.

Each of us has a choice about the outcome of our future, based on each "moment of action" previous to that future (or present) "moment of event." If these "moments of actions" can be measured in some way mathematically, it is possible that we will be able to truly measure the negative or positive harvests of future "moments of events." Of course, there are many factors to be considered. One of the most important of these is time.

Consider the following rules:

> Time always moves forward. Each moment is unique.
>
> The measurement of time is relative to human perception.
>
> Each moment of time (pocket of light photons) is completely different from the immediate previous one.
>
> Our ability to perceive the Universe is totally limited by our response to light (photons) and its speed.

Because of the above facts, we have no choice but to use our measurement of time as best as we perceive it. In this book, we will measure time in the present conventional way as scientists do, such as the year, the month, the day, the hour, the minute, the second, the photon and a particle of light. In terms of time, your actual birth to death time can be measured in many ways.

You must also be aware that...

The YEAR is determined by the Earth's orbit around the Sun.

The MONTH is determined by the Moon's orbit around the Earth.

The DAY is determined by the rotation of the Earth on its axis.

The HOUR is a standard division of the day into 24 parts.

The MINUTE is an hour divided into 60 parts.

The SECOND is a minute divided into 60 parts.

The PHOTON is an atomic particle and a property of light.

The TACHYONS are particles with speeds exceeding light.

Please note that most of these do not agree totally, but together they are used for measuring time. So, to be able to agree with today's conventional rules of time measurement, we are forced to use the positions of the Sun and Moon as the standard time constants in all our calculations.

Chapter 2

What are Vedic Codes?
How are They Important to You?

First, you need to understand how Vedic codes are calculated or developed. Vedic codes are derived from Vedic mathematics. Vedic mathematics is a science of numbers that summarizes the values and measurements of all things in the Universe using the numbers between 0 and 9. This form of math considers any number above the number 9 a repetition of the numbers between 0 and 9.

The concept of human life is determined in what we call levels or forms. The numbers above 9 are referred to in Vedic science as a higher level of the same numbers below 9. For example, the number 18 is considered a higher level of 9(1+8).

The basic form of this mathematical science is the addition of numbers horizontally instead of vertically. It views all numbers larger then 9 as multiples of any number under the value of 9. For example, if we look at the number 11 in Vedic mathematics, it would be considered as the number 2, by adding sideways the numbers 1+1. Similarly, the number 33 would be considered a Vedic code of 6.

As you can see, any number no matter how large or small in value can be brought down to a Vedic code between zero and nine. For example, take a number of 3,563 and add the digits 3+5+6+3 the result will be 17 and if we further add the 1+7, we will obtain the Vedic Code of 8.

Please note also that the number 9 is the number of completion and termination. After every 9 level, the other number contains a 0 such as 20 after 19 or 30 after 29 and so on. Also, if you add any number to the number

9, the Vedic math result would be the same number. For example 9 plus 12 gives the result 21. Both 12 & 21 adds up to Vedic Code 3. Another example is if 9 is added to the number 50 (9+5+0) it would again result in the number 5 as if you had just added 5+0 and got 5. As you can see the number 9 is a complete number.

Periods, dashes, commas and slashes are not recognized as part of Vedic mathematics. Decimals are considered a Western method of number partitions whereas in Vedic mathematics, only the "whole" of anything is recognized, not fractions or percentages. In the Vedic Code of Science, when there is part of a whole (fractions), it is considered a whole number by itself. For example, take a look at your house address, which might be 150-44 Magnolia Street. The dash is ignored, and the numbers are added, as follows: 1+5+0+4+4=14=1+4= the Vedic Code of 5.

Another example is your birthday, which is written in the Western system as follows, 2/12/1962. The Vedic Code for the month and day (ignoring the slashes) is 2+1+2=5 and the Vedic Code for the year of birth is 1+9+6+2=18=1+8 = 9.

In this book, we refer to the House Number Code as the Location Code, and we refer to your Birth Month and Day Code as your Birth Code. Your year of birth is not considered to be part of your Birth Code but is separately called your Karmic Code.

There are many other codes, which we will be considering in this book, such as:

Δ The Birth Code
Δ The Death Code
Δ The Sexual Code
Δ The Love Code
Δ The Wealth Code
Δ The Childbirth Code
Δ The Career Code

Δ The Car Code
Δ The Meditation Code
Δ The Family Code
And so on...

There are hundreds of codes that can be linked to your Birth Code, which explains why you can experience certain events in your life such as accidents, sicknesses, profits and success. With the help of these Vedic Codes, a person can plan, predict and successfully complete a happy lifestyle. This knowledge can have a geometric effect on the Universe, making all people successful and happy.

I will make an attempt to cover most of the basic Vedic Codes in this book, but it is most certain that I have to provide this unique and interesting knowledge in a series of volumes, which hopefully I will be able to do in the next few years.

The first five numbers from 0 to 4 are considered Fixed Vedic Codes and the next five numbers from 5 to 9 are considered Variable Vedic Codes. This simply means that the last five codes have changeable effects whereas the first five codes have fixed effect on the Universe. There are many types of meanings and interpretations to the Vedic Codes 0 to 9; however, we present in this book only some of the important codes that the people of the world need to know now for their own prosperity.

The major effects of the Vedic Codes are given as follows:

The Vedic Code of Science for #1 – The Forces of Creativity & Renewal

The Vedic Code of Science for #2 – The Forces of Love & Beauty

The Vedic Code of Science for #3 – The Forces of Birth & Knowledge

The Vedic Code of Science for #4 – The Forces of Work & Structure

The Vedic Code of Science for #5 – The Forces of Sexuality & Change

The Vedic Code of Science for #6 – The Forces of Power & Destruction

The Vedic Code of Science for #7 – The Forces of Spirituality & Mysticism

The Vedic Code of Science for #8 – The Forces of Materiality & Wealth

The Vedic Code of Science for #9 – The Forces of Termination & Death

To simplify our system of interpretation, I have added a key name to each Vedic code and so we refer to these codes throughout by the names as shown below given to each code from one to nine.

CODE	KEY NAMES		KEY WORD
1	Brahma	Jesus	Creator
2	Durga	Mary	Love
3	Vishnu	Solomon	Birth
4	Rudra	Abraham	Work
5	Narayan	Gabriel	Change
6	Kali	Saul	Destruction
7	Shiva	Solomon	Spirituality
8	Laxmi	Moses	Wealth
9	Indra	Elijah	Death

Before I introduce how the system of Vedic codes can explain and improve your life, I will show you how the Vedic Code of Science has been applied to recent world events, as well as incidents of significance that have changed the way of all life on Earth. Looking at the World Trade Center destruction, I decided to use this as my example of how the Vedic Code can provide acceptable explanations of a certain event.

We all believe that destiny is fixed, but that is not the view of Vedic science. Free will is predominant in the Universe; we all have choices to make on our path in life. We can decide freely between a choice of good or evil. However, one must remember that the Universe is a self-preserving, just like a living person is self-preserving.

If an individual chooses evil, then the Universe will move towards protecting itself from that evil by creating destructive events. If the choice is good, then the Universe will move towards promoting the entity for continuous existence in the world.

Every human being has a choice to become prosperous as long as the universal rules of preservation and creation are observed. Life is a path of choices and in every moment of time we are given an opportunity to choose.

Chapter 3

The Vedic Science Rules of
Natural Action & Reaction

Free will is determined by the choice and action we take at the moment the choice is given. The reaction to the action we have taken is the result of the choice that was freely chosen in a previous moment is the essence of free will.

Many times we say, "Well, if I had not been there, it would not have happened." Did you ever consider the fact that it was a previous action or moment that lead you to this important moment? A closer look at this would reveal a chain of events that led to that important moment in time. It is obvious that each moment of action predetermines the next moment of experience.

Hence I have come up with the following rules about future events:

The Vedic Code of Science Rule #1

All our actions determine the path toward future experiences.

The moment of an experience or event is either negative or positive, preceded by a negative or positive decision, according to the path taken prior to that moment of event or experience.

Even though, at any given space, time or moment of experience, there is a design in which any arrangement of atomic particles is possible, it is true that no pattern of arrangement will appear exactly the same way twice. Ever.

But, sometimes, even though events bring good or bad experiences in our lives, we sometimes wish that we had made a different decision in one of the "moments of actions" previous to the one made just moments earlier. Hence, we experience regret or disappointment, which could lead to further negative moments.

For example, a man decides to get drunk after being disappointed. However, if at that moment he decides not to drink, but to be positive about what had happened that led to his disappointment, he could change his future "moments of experiences" or events.

The Vedic Code of Science Rule #2

Time is not arbitrary. At every moment in a creature's life or progress, many crossroads are confronted with a free choice as to which one to take. A different future experience or event lies on the path of each crossroad.

Each crossroad leads to a different future, all of them fixed and all of them possible, ready to become part of one's experience or "path of events." Many times people cannot decide on a path because, based on their "past actions", they will not make a decision as to which path to follow next. A decision, whether correct or not, will lead to a whole number of future events or experiences that may turn out to be beneficial or not, i.e., negative or positive.

The Vedic Code of Science Rule #3

The future is an infinite reservoir of an infinite number of future events or experiences, each of them fixed, yet malleable or changeable, depending on the path chosen by the body or mass intended for that experience.

Your layer of experience, as a result of your decision, will be along a certain path, which will be a completely different layer of experience than if you had chosen a different path or made a different decision.

Each of us has a vision of the world that belongs to us alone. Others will share in some parts of it, but none will see it exactly as you do, nor will everyone experience it the same way. Each person's vision of reality is based upon his or her life experience, the influence of people, the environment, books, dreams, etc. Our thinking has been channeled into paths assumed to be the only avenues of progress. However, if there were other paths that were better, of which we do not know or did not choose somewhere in time, we might be quite unaware of different methodologies or experiences of progress, which may be more advantageous. We could have chosen any one of those paths.

The Vedic Code of Science Rule #4

The Isaac Newton concept of physics, for example, was completely affected and revised by Albert Einstein's theories. Now quantum theories indicate that some of Einstein's theories were incorrect. No doubt what is accepted as truth today could very well be proven tomorrow to be only amusing. Prevailing opinions often affect established theories. No one goes to his or her death willingly. Each of us believes in a selfish way that he or she will survive. Each of us is not only a participant, but also an observer.

Ours is a world that has developed along mechanistic lines, but is it possible that there may be other ways. Perhaps dozens of other ways, unknown because of the one that we found that worked.

The quantum theory injects strange new possibilities into our narrow world. In a more prospective sense, our three dimensional world is so comfortable that the possibility of a much greater reality is disturbing to us. Quantum theory shows that our school of general thinking is cluttered with beliefs long proved absurd by contemporary knowledge. Man has demonstrated over and over again that the last thing he needs are new ideas, even when they are desperately needed!

Most theories are merely dancing shadows against a hard wall of reality. How few answers we possess of phenomena that go beyond our reality to explain it or understand it! Thus Earth's orbit around the Sun is not equal to one year. There is a 0.25 difference. The circle of 360 degrees is not equal to one revolution of the Earth in 24 hours. Last but not least, the orbit of the Moon is not exactly 30 days. What time is it, really? You decide for yourself.

Chapter 4

Special Attention to
Vedic Code #9 –
The Vedic Code of Indra

Before we proceed to the next chapters, it is important that you understand the tremendous power of Vedic Code #9. As we discussed in the Introduction, any number added to 9 does not lose its Vedic Code identity. Any number that is a multiple of 9 retains its identity as 9, also. The number 9 can have a tremendously negative effect on a situation or an extremely positive effect depending on the connection or path it is related to. Many famous criminals have Birth Code #9.

Six hundred and sixty-six (666) adds to 18, which adds to 9, which symbolizes (at least) a tremendous number of curiously similar coincidences.

A Great Sidereal Year is 25,920 years. This is how long it takes for all the planets to return to their same positions and relationships to each other. It has to do with the precessions of the equinoxes. This means that spring and fall equinoxes occur just a fraction earlier each year. It takes 72 years to complete one degree of equinoctial advance (7+2=9).

If you add the digits of the Great Sidereal Year, you find they also equate to 18 – and, of course, 1+8=9. Two and a half degrees of equinoctial precession occur in 180 years (1+8+0=9), a period, which cycle experts have shown to be extremely important in political changes.

In the monthly bulletin of the New Jersey Astrologers Association, editor George J. McCormack published many series of cosmological cycles, all of which equate to the number 9 – and to man. "The added digits of various cosmic cycles," he wrote in the November 1958 issue of ASTROTECH, "when reduced to 9 show a striking relationship between macrocosmic and microcosmic cycles. The Grand Year of Equinoctial Precession – 25,920 years – equates to 18 or 9. The 360 degrees of the zodiac and of terrestrial longitude also equate to 9. Whether you add all the minutes in a day (1,440) or all the seconds (86,400), the digits always add to nine. One degree of equinoctial advance takes 72 years."

Any number of degrees of equinoctial precession equates to 9! Two degrees take 144 years; 3 degrees take 270 years; 10 degrees, 720 years; 5 degrees, 360 years. Or the entire 360 degrees of precession take 25,920 years – both of which, as we have seen, equal 9.

The mean normal respiration rate in humans is 18 times a minute; the normal human heart beat or pulse rate is 72 times a minute. Both equate to nine. The average number of heartbeats in one hour comes to 4,320 – or 9. The average number of breaths in an hour is 1,080 – also 9. In 24 hours the heart beats an average of 103,680 times, all which add to 18 or 9.

It takes 270 days or 9 months to complete the period of human gestation. Is this also a coincidence? It hardly seem coincidental that the harmonious angel of 30 degrees, 60 degrees, 120 degrees and 150 degrees formed between planets equate either 3 or 6, while the adverse or discordant aspects of 45 degrees, 90 degrees, 135 degrees and 180 degrees, each total 9!

Historians and cycle experts have concluded that great political, dynastic, and historical changes occur in cycles, which all equate to 9. These are exactly the number of years during which any number of degrees (or fractions thereof) of equinoctial precession take place. It takes 2,160 years for the equinoxes to proceed through 30 degrees of the zodiac or 1 sign. The equinoxes proceed through the 90-degree (3 signs) in 6,480 years. It moves one half of a degree in 36 years, a quarter of a degree in 18 years, and eighth of a degree in 9 years.

The 6,480-year period (3 signs) is kabalistically called an Age, and the centers of world civilization have gradually moved westward in phase with this precession. Ancient records of the cradle of Western civilization indicate that these 6,480-year cycles are traditionally believed to end in global catastrophe.

One of these kabalistic observations was that the reduced sum of all digits is 9. Thus, 1, 2, 3, 4, 5, 6, 7, 8, and 9 added together equals 45 (4+5=9). *Nine is the basis of the unit value of all numbers!*

Nine is also the fantastic number that figured in the death of Maximilian, emperor of Mexico – and in the silver peso that was coined in his honor. He reigned for three short years, between 1864 and 1867. When the last coinage was struck during his reign, the die broke. The last piece was badly mangled, and there hangs the thread of a fantastic story: as soon as the die broke, a tiny chip (something like a gash) appeared on Maximilian's forehead. As each peso was minted, the crack grew a little bigger and the die became progressively worse. By the time the 32nd piece was minted, the damage was clearly evident. (Maximilian was only 32 years old when he became emperor.)

The next three coins were badly broken, and the final (36th) piece was mangled almost beyond recognition. Indian workmen took this as an omen that the emperor would die violently of a head wound at the age of 36 – killed either by a sword or bullet wound. The American officer in charge of the Mint rejected the Aztec, Miztec and Toltec superstitions of his Indio workmen, but they were right!

Napoleon III placed Ferdinand Joseph Maximilian, brother of the emperor of Austria, on Mexico's throne on June 12, 1864. Despite appearances, Maximilian was a true humanitarian, who really wanted to help the Mexicans. But he was executed on June 19, 1867, at the age of 36. Bullets horribly mangled his whole body but only one bullet entered his head – and at the exact spot designated by the chip, which appeared on his likeness on the silver peso! Was this the power of 9 operating in his life?

All cultures in all history reflect this value of 9 as adverse to human kind on this planet. The 144,000 saints gathered from the 12 tribes of Israel equals 9. The Masonic Order of the "Elect of Nine" incorporates 9 roses, 9 lights and 9 knocks in the ceremony.

Ancient Jews were forbidden to wear either the Talleth or the Phylacteries on the 9th day of the month of Ab. In the story of the Kilhiveh and Alwen, the castle was built with 9 gates and 9 portals beside which sat 9 dogs. King Arthur symbolically fought an enchanted pig (his baser nature) for 9 days and 9 nights.

Receiving the Holy Eucharist on the first Fridays of 9 consecutive months is believed by Roman Catholics to be assurance of dying in a state of grace. Novenas are celebrated for 9 consecutive days.

In Grecian mythology there are 9 Muses, the daughters of Jupiter and Mnemosyne (memory). When Roman male infants were 9 days old, a Feast of Purification was held for them. Romans were buried on the 9th day. A "Novennalia" or Feast of Death was held for the deceased every 9th year.

There are 9 mother Goddesses in Hinduism. A woman is considered perfect when she is able to perform the 9 functions of a woman in life. Most of the Gods in Hinduism are considered to have 9 different functions or forms. The deity known as Ganesh has 9 forms and is considered the Remover of Obstacles.

The most interesting correlation to the #9 is the goddess of wealth in Hinduism called Laxmi. She is considered the white light that exists in our Universe, and it is stated in the Vedic text that Laxmi has 9 forms, which can be exactly compared to the 9 forms of electromagnetic energy found in the white light coming from the Sun.

This includes the 7 colors of the rainbow that we see as well as the 2 we don't see – ultraviolet and infrared.

The #9 is the number of Yamraj, the God of Death and also represents the Hindu God Dharamraj, the God of Truth. The God of Death is considered the guardian of hell and burial grounds. It may appear to be coincidence that you will find most burial grounds are on a street that adds up to a 9 or at an address that adds up to a 9. The location where truth is tested and tried – courthouses – usually have addresses that add up to the #9.

Famous missionaries, priests, great swamis and gurus, such as SAI BABA, have Birth Codes that add up to the #9. One of the most loved U. S. presidents, Bill Clinton, has a Birth Code of 9.

Due to its highest position in the number system it is considered the limit at which our present Universe ends and the next Universe begins. It is the limiting point between parallel universes. After the 9th form of electromagnetic energy, which is the limit of the speed of light, the Universe enters into another dimension where no laws of physics are able to work.

Because of its encompassing effect on life in the Universe, the #9 is closest to God, but also closest to 0, the companion of what is considered negative or evil; thus in Vedic Science, we see 9 and multiples of 9 occurring frequently in the Vedic scriptures.

There are 18 (1+8=9) chapters in the Bhagavad Gita. A normal person takes 21,600 (2+1+6=9) breaths in day. There are 792,000 (7+9+2=18, 1+8=9) nadis or energy centers in the human body. Vedic hymns are written in meters of 9. However, like the odometer on a car, when the highest level of 9 is reached, it rolls over to 0 to begin its cycle all over again.

Because of this proximity or closeness to 0, the number 9 is also farthest from God. Thus 9 acts with confusion in its normal state because it does not know if it belongs to God or to Yama (God of Death). If it is well grounded and follows the Sattvic path (path of goodness) consistently, 9 can achieve the highest level of spirituality. If it follows the Tamasic path (path of ignorance and darkness), 9 can end up in the deepest levels of Patal (Hell). It is because of this multiplicity of behavior that confusion reigns in our true understanding of this number.

John Lennon: How the #9 Affected His Life

John Lennon, the musician and songwriter, believed in the influence of the #9. He was born on October 9, 1940. His mother's house was 9 Newcastle Road in Liverpool, where John wrote at least three songs with 9 in the title. "One after 909," "Revolution No. 9," and "#9 Dream." The song "Imagine" starts with the 9th letter of the alphabet. The Impresario Brian Epstein first saw the Beatles perform live when he attended one of their lunchtime gigs at the Cavern in Liverpool on November 9, 1961. He quickly became their manager, signing their EMI Parlophone record deal on May 9, 1962.

The Beatles' first song, "Love Me Do", had the number 4949. John Lennon first met Yoko Ono on November 9, 1966. The Beatles' legal partnership was ended on January 9, 1975. John and Yoko's son Sean was born on John's birthday, October 9 1975. They lived in an apartment on West 72nd Street, New York (7+2=9). Their apartment number in the Dakota building was also 72 (9).

John was shot and killed just outside that building on the evening of December 8, 1980, when it was December 9 back in Liverpool. His body was taken to a hospital on 9th Avenue. Using only the consonants of Beatle, the number comes to 'his' number, 9. Using only the consonants of Lennon, the number comes to 18, 1+8=9. Add the two – 9+9=18, 1+8=9 – and we have the numinous power of 9 reproducing and just as supernaturally returning us to Lennon's birth number.

Chapter 5

Cases That Prove the
Vedic Code of Science

Case Histories of People with Similar Birthdates
This chapter is dedicated to some interesting evidence of the Vedic Code of Science's successful application. The following cases clearly prove that the Vedic Code of Science works and can be used as a Life Consulting Science. The source of the information below came from the book, *New Age Science*, by Robert F. Goodavage, who is credited with great research in proving that the Universe has order and is really a living Universe.

A Strange Incident Involving the Name Peterson
In April 1958, another strange incident involving variations on the name "Peterson" occurred outside Miami, Florida. Three cars were stopped at a red light when a young woman rammed the last car from behind. Here was the lineup:

Cecil H. Peterson drove car No. 1.
Harry C. Petterson drove Car No. 2.
Arthur H. Pettersen drove Car No. 3.

All three cars suffered similar damage. It was reported that Peterson, Petterson and Pettersen were born in different years – but all within four days of the same month. None was related to any of the others.

Birth and Death at the Same Moment
The bizarre and unexplainable case of Donald Chapman and Donald Brazil is representative of about 10 others of its kind. They were born at the same hour and minute in neighboring towns in California on September 5, 1933.

Five days after their 23rd birthday – on September 10, 1956 – Donald Brazil of Ferndale and Donald Chapman of Eureka met for the first and last time in this life as they drove in opposite directions on U.S. Highway 101, south of Eureka, early on a Sunday morning. They crashed head on, and both were killed instantly.

Don Brazil and Don Chapman, who were born at the same moment and lived nearly identical lives, held the same kind of jobs and dated girls in each other's hometowns, also died at the same moment – each causing the other's death. Was it just another meaningless coincidence? Astrologers claim the planetary patterns in the horoscopes of parents and grandparents are reflected in the charts of their offspring.

In this particular case, it is worthy to note that Donald Brazil's father was killed in an automobile accident at the same place on the same road on September 10, 1954 (See AP report, September 10, 1956, Eureka, CA.)

The Fantastic "Coincidence" in Ireland
Shortly before Christmas, about three months after the deaths of Don Brazil and Don Chapman in 1956, Jack Smith and his wife were driving along a road in Dublin next to the River Liffey that flows through the Irish capital. In a rare accident, their car somehow flipped off the road and toppled into the river.

Mr. and Mrs. Jack Smith were drowned. Their children, 11-year-old Vicky and 8-year-old Peter (who were not with them) became orphans – but not for long. John Shannon and his wife, close friends of the Smiths, adopted the children. Four years from the date, on which the Smiths had drowned, John Shannon was driving along the same road. Somehow, his car slipped off the road and toppled into the River Liffey at the exact spot the Smiths' car had gone down. Shannon had also drowned. He left a widow and two orphans – Peter and Vicky. John Shannon was born in the same year and month and only four days after the birth of Jack Smith!

Firemen, Policemen, and Mars
On July 19, 1913, Michael J. Murphy and Edward Thompson were born in Queens County, New York. Unknown to the other, each boy had similar interests and ambitions. Each graduated from Brooklyn Law School in the Class of 1936, but future events transpired with about a year's difference in their lives.

Since astrology claims Mars is associated with firemen and policemen, and since Mars was prominent in their respective horoscopes, it is interesting to note that Michael J. Murphy rose through the ranks to become police commissioner of the world's greatest city, while Edward Thompson became the same city's fire commissioner.

Another California Tragedy
Thirty-one years after Murphy and Thompson were born; two other boys came into the world at the same time on the West Coast. The common birthdate of Fred Schokley Jr. and Barrett Woodruff was July 19, 1944. They were close friends through elementary and high school, and they had identical grades, identical interests, hobbies, likes and dislikes. They did the same things at the same time and entered Oakland City College together.

On March 23, 1964, after taking home their dates, they headed for Oakland for a late snack. Neither boy made it. Each smashed into a trailer truck, each was thrown from his car, and each suffered identical fatal injuries – each died at the same moment. Some "coincidence"!

The Fugitive "Twins"
On February 27, 1964, another remarkable coincidence occurred in two different states at the same time. In

Hackettstown, NJ, a 17-year-old escapee from Annandale Reformatory held off state and local police from the attic of an abandoned house during a two-hour gun battle. The fugitive fired a .22 caliber rifle, but had a shotgun and some pistols as well. Troopers brought in tear gas, but the boy's father managed to talk him into surrendering.

On the same date and hour in Syracuse, N.Y. another 17-year-old boy was holding off police and state troopers from another attic retreat – also with a .22 caliber rifle. He too had other weapons. This boy's father tried to talk him down, but was unsuccessful. The boy was smoked out with a barrage of tear gas.

Both boys were born in the same year, same month and same date.

The "Astro-Twin" Families
In 1939 two unrelated women met for the first time in a hospital room in Hackensack, NJ. Their last names were Hanna and Osborne, but they had the same first name – Edna. Each woman had a baby at the same time; the babies weighed the same and were given the same name – Patricia Edna. Just another coincidence, maybe, but here's what their conversation revealed – both their husbands were named Harold. Each Harold was in the same business and owned the same make, model and color car.

The Hannas and the Osbornes had been married exactly three-and-a-half years and had the same anniversary. The babies were their first. Both fathers were born in the same year, month and day. The mothers too had the same birthdate – and the same number of brothers and sisters. Each Edna was a blue-eyed brunette – same height and same weight – and wore the same size clothes.

Their husbands were of the same religion – different than that of their wives, which also had the same. Each

27

family owned a dog, named Spot – same mixed breed, same size and same age. Both Spots were bought at the same time and were of the same sex.

The Obvious is the Most Difficult to See

On March 30, 1964, a doctor and his wife were sentenced to two years in prison in Tucson, AZ for extreme cruelty to their five-year-old adopted daughter, Tina. The housekeeper found the child – beaten, bloody, and half-starved. Her hands were tightly roped behind her back, and she cowered behind the furnace room in the basement. The shocked housekeeper released the child and called police, who were obliged to protect their prisoners against a mob of outraged neighbors.

At almost the same time, but in another state, an identical story unfolded. A dentist and his wife had beaten and brutalized their five-year-old adopted daughter and kept her tied up in the basement of their home. They too were sentenced. The second child was Tina's twin sister from whom she had been separated since infancy!

Coincidences – Chance or Fate? By Ken Anderson

President Ronald Reagan and Vedic Code #7

According to Robert Ripley in *The Book of Chances* (1989), former President Ronald Reagan saved 77 people from drowning during his 7 years as a lifeguard at a resort near Dixon, IL. The book uses this as a starting point to show how the number 7 kept cropping up in Reagan's life.

He celebrated his 70th birthday 17 days after his first inauguration. John Hinckley wounded Reagan on his 70th day in office. The bullet fired by Hinckley ricocheted off Reagan's 7th rib.

Reagan made his film debut in 1937 and became president of the Screen Actors' Guild in 1947. He began his term as governor of California in 1967 and was re-elected in 1970. His formal acceptance speech for the

Republican presidential nomination was made on the 17th day of the 7th month 1980. At the end of his second term in the White House he was 77.

President Abraham Lincoln and Vedic Code #7

Significant 7 has long been attributed to Abraham Lincoln – the 16th (1+6=7) president of the US. Even if the following does stretch credulity, it shows one way of tracing a pattern of a personal number. Each of Lincoln's names contains 7 letters. He lived 7 years in Kentucky and 7 years in Salem. In the army he was a private (7 letters) and a captain (7).

Lincoln was elected 7 times, sworn into Congress on 7 December 1847, held 7 offices in succession. His ancestors came from Hingham (7 letters), in Norfolk (7 letters), England (7 letters). He served 7 years in the state legislature. He appointed 7 cabinet ministers, watched 7 states secede and died a few minutes after 7 on the 7th day.

President Thomas Jefferson and Vedic Code #3

The number 3 dogged the 3rd U. S. president. Thomas Jefferson was born 13 April 1743, the 3rd child and the 3rd Thomas in the family. He became the 3rd president, but not before he largely wrote the Declaration of Independence at the age of 33. And not before he lost the 1796 election by 3 votes. Jefferson died at the age of 83 on 4 July 1826, the 50th anniversary of American Independence.

Another American president also died on that date: John Adams, the 2nd president. Incidentally, 4 July was significant for yet another president, Calvin Coolidge, the 30th president, who was born on 4 July 1872.

Time Twins

On 7 November 1984, Gail McClure and her sister, Carl Killian, gave birth to daughters within an hour of each other at Mesa's Lutheran Hospital in Arizona. Three years later they did it again at the same hospital. On 11 February 1987, Gail had a son, Benjamin. Forty-five minutes later, Carol had another girl, Christi, when the same doctor, who had delivered the first babies, carried out a Caesarian section.

"After we did it the first time, we talked about doing it again," said Gail. "We tried to plan the due date in March but both got pregnant sooner. Then we didn't talk about it, because we both thought we had ruined the plan." It wasn't until they were both three months pregnant that they found out both were due at the same time again. Gail was due on 1 February and Carol a week later. 'She waited for me,' said Carol. 'Is that amazing or what?'

Kerrie, Kerry

And yet another variation, also full of coincidences – Two women with almost the same name gave birth on the same day, both two weeks early, on 31 March 1988, prompting people who first heard the story to talk of an April Fool's joke.

The two women – Kerry Mason and Kerrie Mason – live within five kilometers of each another. Both women had boys, and they had the same doctor. Confirmation of the details came from the two women, their gynecologists and the hospitals in which they gave birth. Neither knew the other before the births but were put in touch by their doctors, who said the women were expected to give birth within two days of each other, but both went into labor two weeks early.

Dead on Time

Yet another time twin story – In New York a furniture manufacturer named Richardson met by chance a man named Negrelli, who looked exactly like him. Negrelli was born in Italy on Richardson's birthday. Four days after the chance meeting, Richardson was run over by a car and died two days later. In a different part of the city,

Negrelli had been run over by a car and, though this had been two weeks earlier, both Negrelli and Richardson died on the same day as a result of their injuries.

Unknown Mates

Here is a case of two mothers, who had never met; yet they gave birth to children on the same dates, twice. On 5 May 1981, Denise Weldon and Cheryl Tynan gave birth at the Baptist Medical Center in Birmingham, AL. Weldon had a boy and Tynan, a girl.

Twenty-three months later they were back at the same hospital and gave birth again almost at the same time. This time Weldon had a girl and Tynan, a boy. Dr. Ronald Goldberg delivered all four children. Both women had visited him, usually on Mondays, during their pregnancies and both had visited him on the Monday before the birth. Neither of them had ever met.

Chapter 6

The Vedic Birth Code –
The Key to Your Existence

Just like your fingerprints, everyone has a birthday code that can never be duplicated with the same name. This forms a unique code since no person born on the same day will have the same name; if they do, they will have similar experiences in life.

As you saw by the cases in Chapter 5, people with similar birthdates can experience the same events in their lives, and more so when their birthdates and names are similar. The Vedic Code of Science recognizes that a person's birthdate marks the beginning of their lifeline, and so it is regarded highly as a coordinate point that can determine the direction and the path that the lifeline of the person will take. The Vedic Code also recognizes that the name of a person determines the characteristics of the person's lifeline as they proceed from birth towards death. This chapter is restricted to information about the birthday code.

The foundation of your life is embedded in the Birth Code itself. This code is used as a base number to determine how every other code affects your life in terms of achievements, objectives, beliefs, emotions and more. It will explain your relationships with others, your marriage, love life, your likes and dislikes. It will determine the kind of career you follow, the type of car you should buy for success, the type of colors suited best for you, the type of jewelry you should use for success and more. The Birth Code will advise you when to travel safely, when you should have children, when you should buy a house for success, what address is lucky for you and where you should buy it...and more

To find your birthday code, the following table has been provided. Each birthdate from January 1 to December 31 is included in the table. Against each month and day of birth, you will find the Vedic Code that matches that day of birth. This number or code will be referred to as your Birth Code.

TABLE 6:1 - BIRTHDAYS vs. VEDIC BIRTH CODE

01-Jan	2	27-Jan	1	22-Feb	6	19-Mar	4	14-Apr	9
02-Jan	3	28-Jan	2	23-Feb	7	20-Mar	5	15-Apr	1
03-Jan	4	29-Jan	3	24-Feb	8	21-Mar	6	16-Apr	2
04-Jan	5	30-Jan	4	25-Feb	9	22-Mar	7	17-Apr	3
05-Jan	6	31-Jan	5	26-Feb	1	23-Mar	8	18-Apr	4
06-Jan	7	01-Feb	3	27-Feb	2	24-Mar	9	19-Apr	5
07-Jan	8	02-Feb	4	28-Feb	3	25-Mar	1	20-Apr	6
08-Jan	9	03-Feb	5	29-Feb	4	26-Mar	2	21-Apr	7
09-Jan	1	04-Feb	6	01-Mar	4	27-Mar	3	22-Apr	8
10-Jan	2	05-Feb	7	02-Mar	5	28-Mar	4	23-Apr	9
11-Jan	3	06-Feb	8	03-Mar	6	29-Mar	5	24-Apr	1
12-Jan	4	07-Feb	9	04-Mar	7	30-Mar	6	25-Apr	2
13-Jan	5	08-Feb	1	05-Mar	8	31-Mar	7	26-Apr	3
14-Jan	6	09-Feb	2	06-Mar	9	01-Apr	5	27-Apr	4
15-Jan	7	10-Feb	3	07-Mar	1	02-Apr	6	28-Apr	5
16-Jan	8	11-Feb	4	08-Mar	2	03-Apr	7	29-Apr	6
17-Jan	9	12-Feb	5	09-Mar	3	04-Apr	8	30-Apr	7
18-Jan	1	13-Feb	6	10-Mar	4	05-Apr	9	01-May	6
19-Jan	2	14-Feb	7	11-Mar	5	06-Apr	1	02-May	7
20-Jan	3	15-Feb	8	12-Mar	6	07-Apr	2	03-May	8
21-Jan	4	16-Feb	9	13-Mar	7	08-Apr	3	04-May	9
22-Jan	5	17-Feb	1	14-Mar	8	09-Apr	4	05-May	1
23-Jan	6	18-Feb	2	15-Mar	9	10-Apr	5	06-May	2
24-Jan	7	19-Feb	3	16-Mar	1	11-Apr	6	07-May	3
25-Jan	8	20-Feb	4	17-Mar	2	12-Apr	7	08-May	4
26-Jan	9	21-Feb	5	18-Mar	3	13-Apr	8	09-May	5

TABLE 6:1 - BIRTHDAYS vs. VEDIC BIRTH CODE

10-May	6	11-Jun	8	13-Jul	2	14-Aug	4	15-Sep	6
11-May	7	12-Jun	9	14-Jul	3	15-Aug	5	16-Sep	7
12-May	8	13-Jun	1	15-Jul	4	16-Aug	6	17-Sep	8
13-May	9	14-Jun	2	16-Jul	5	17-Aug	7	18-Sep	9
14-May	1	15-Jun	3	17-Jul	6	18-Aug	8	19-Sep	1
15-May	2	16-Jun	4	18-Jul	7	19-Aug	9	20-Sep	2
16-May	3	17-Jun	5	19-Jul	8	20-Aug	1	21-Sep	3
17-May	4	18-Jun	6	20-Jul	9	21-Aug	2	22-Sep	4
18-May	5	19-Jun	7	21-Jul	1	22-Aug	3	23-Sep	5
19-May	6	20-Jun	8	22-Jul	2	23-Aug	4	24-Sep	6
20-May	7	21-Jun	9	23-Jul	3	24-Aug	5	25-Sep	7
21-May	8	22-Jun	1	24-Jul	4	25-Aug	6	26-Sep	8
22-May	9	23-Jun	2	25-Jul	5	26-Aug	7	27-Sep	9
23-May	1	24-Jun	3	26-Jul	6	27-Aug	8	28-Sep	1
24-May	2	25-Jun	4	27-Jul	7	28-Aug	9	29-Sep	2
25-May	3	26-Jun	5	28-Jul	8	29-Aug	1	30-Sep	3
26-May	4	27-Jun	6	29-Jul	9	30-Aug	2	01-Oct	2
27-May	5	28-Jun	7	30-Jul	1	31-Aug	3	02-Oct	3
28-May	6	29-Jun	8	31-Jul	2	01-Sep	1	03-Oct	4
29-May	7	30-Jun	9	01-Aug	9	02-Sep	2	04-Oct	5
30-May	8	01-Jul	8	02-Aug	1	03-Sep	3	05-Oct	6
31-May	9	02-Jul	9	03-Aug	2	04-Sep	4	06-Oct	7
01-Jun	7	03-Jul	1	04-Aug	3	05-Sep	5	07-Oct	8
02-Jun	8	04-Jul	2	05-Aug	4	06-Sep	6	08-Oct	9
03-Jun	9	05-Jul	3	06-Aug	5	07-Sep	7	09-Oct	1
04-Jun	1	06-Jul	4	07-Aug	6	08-Sep	8	10-Oct	2
05-Jun	2	07-Jul	5	08-Aug	7	09-Sep	9	11-Oct	3
06-Jun	3	08-Jul	6	09-Aug	8	10-Sep	1	12-Oct	4
07-Jun	4	09-Jul	7	10-Aug	9	11-Sep	2	13-Oct	5
08-Jun	5	10-Jul	8	11-Aug	1	12-Sep	3	14-Oct	6
09-Jun	6	11-Jul	9	12-Aug	2	13-Sep	4	15-Oct	7
10-Jun	7	12-Jul	1	13-Aug	3	14-Sep	5	16-Oct	8

TABLE 6:1 - BIRTHDAYS vs. VEDIC BIRTH CODE									
17-Oct	9	02-Nov	4	18-Nov	2	04-Dec	7	20-Dec	5
18-Oct	1	03-Nov	5	19-Nov	3	05-Dec	8	21-Dec	6
19-Oct	2	04-Nov	6	20-Nov	4	06-Dec	9	22-Dec	7
20-Oct	3	05-Nov	7	21-Nov	5	07-Dec	1	23-Dec	8
21-Oct	4	06-Nov	8	22-Nov	6	08-Dec	2	24-Dec	9
22-Oct	5	07-Nov	9	23-Nov	7	09-Dec	3	25-Dec	1
23-Oct	6	08-Nov	1	24-Nov	8	10-Dec	4	26-Dec	2
24-Oct	7	09-Nov	2	25-Nov	9	11-Dec	5	27-Dec	3
25-Oct	8	10-Nov	3	26-Nov	1	12-Dec	6	28-Dec	4
26-Oct	9	11-Nov	4	27-Nov	2	13-Dec	7	29-Dec	5
27-Oct	1	12-Nov	5	28-Nov	3	14-Dec	8	30-Dec	6
28-Oct	2	13-Nov	6	29-Nov	4	15-Dec	9	31-Dec	7
29-Oct	3	14-Nov	7	30-Nov	5	16-Dec	1		
30-Oct	4	15-Nov	8	01-Dec	4	17-Dec	2		
31-Oct	5	16-Nov	9	02-Dec	5	18-Dec	3		
01-Nov	3	17-Nov	1	03-Dec	6	19-Dec	4		

Against each birthday, a code is given between 1 and 9. That code from your birthday is going to be used frequently in this chapter and throughout this book whenever a reference to your Birth Code is made to you, the reader.

Table 2 contains key names of Hindu and Christian Gods, which we will refer to as key name codes in this book. This will add more substance to the numeric codes so as to give more life and better meaning to the Vedic Codes mentioned throughout this book.

VEDIC CODES   NAME CODES #1/NAME CODES #2

1	BRAMHA	JESUS
2	DURGA	MARY
3	VISHNU	MOSES
4	GANESH	ABRAHAM
5	NARAYAN	EVE
6	KALI	SAUL
7	SHIVA	SOLOMON
8	LAXMI	DAVID
9	INDRA	ELIJAH

In the following chapter, a brief explanation of your life is written to give you an idea of the importance of the day you began your life. This marks also the beginning point of your lifeline.

During the nine months when your mother carried you in her womb, these karmic effects – together with your genetic codes – were transferred as part of your life. In the chapter called "The Hereditary Code", we will describe how these characteristics are acquired.

Chapter 7

Applying Your Birth Code to Your Life

After finding your Birth Code in the previous chapter, you may now apply it to your life and read the details given for your Birth Code in the following paragraphs. There are 9 Vedic Code interpretations in this chapter and one of them applies to you. Please bear in mind that all of the information provided may not have applied in your life yet, as most of this information covers your whole life.

If you are unmarried then you will not experience some of the qualities of marriage until you grow older. However this book is yours to keep and you can always refer to it later to see if the information has been correct.

Find out which of the following Birth Codes applies to your life and read the interpretations that follow.

Your Life Based on Vedic Birth Code #1
Life According to Bramha

You are independent, lonely sometimes and like to be in charge.

You will achieve high status in career and position in life.

You are very spiritual in your thinking and you think constantly.

You are bossy and commanding in your actions toward others.

You were very lonely and independent as a child.

You always feel that others leave you alone a great deal.

In marriage you should not be too assertive or your independence may result in your partner leaving you for another.

You worry a great deal and this may result in mental nervousness.

As the first number, this represents the origin, the solitary eminence of the Sun, the creator. It is a powerful and creative number, associated with strong masculinity, and people bearing it may become leaders. It refers very much to the self, so people who have it will be individuals with a tendency to be inventive, determined, and possessed of a pioneering spirit. Along with such power must go responsibility, and unless the person is careful, there is a risk of falling into selfishness, egotism, and severe bossiness. If their schemes fail, they may become aggressive or introverted; even if their schemes succeed, they may become overbearing and ruthless.

Karmic Characteristics of Vedic Birth Code #1

At the time of birth, one of your parents was promoted to a leadership position. As a child you were left alone a great deal and may have experienced loneliness being away from your parents. You are a very independent person who does not like to follow others' advice unless it is beneficial to you. Most of the time you like to do your own thing. You may be very controlling and moody. You are unable to follow orders easily and may lead most of your life as a single person. You enjoy being alone sometimes and will specifically take time to contemplate on your opportunities and your emotions. You strive very hard to achieve a high position in career opportunities.

You are willing to study a great deal and may become very dominating in your home. You are required to avoid letting this dominant characteristic affect your relationship as it could result in your being divorced or separated from your lover. If you are unable to submit yourself willingly to be loved by others, your love life may be one of emptiness. Avoid taking people for granted and expecting people to follow your commands. This is a mistake and may create much unhappiness in your life. If you were born at an inauspicious time without proper consultations with priests you may experience much loneliness in life and rejection by all.

Your Life Based on Vedic Birth Code #2
Life According to Durga

You like to shop a great deal and specifically look for bargains.

You are a great cook and will make a great chef at any restaurant.

Any dishes prepared by you will be tasty to others.

You are advised to always serve food to reap good karma.

Feeding anyone who visits your home will bless you with prosperity.

You do not like to deal with work that involves too many calculations.

You have a kind heart and are very helpful to others... sometimes too much.

Others may take advantage of your kindness.

You are a very religious person.

You have a great voice and may become a famous singer.

Marriage may become difficult as a result of illicit affairs.

You receive a great deal of love, but cannot give it.

You are not romantic but like to be romanced by your beloved.

Just as #1 is associated with maleness, so #2 is with femininity, being gentle, intuitive, harmonious and romantic. It is symbolized by the Moon and suggests a mental creativity and an ability to mix well with other people, but an inability to be forceful, to make decisions, or to carry tasks to their necessary conclusions; more mental power than physical.

Karmic Characteristics of Vedic Birth Code #2

You are a kind and generous individual and very true in your feelings for others. You like to assist those that are distressed or those who need help genuinely. You have very few enemies and you are loved by many. Normally according to previous karma, you should be happily married, have a romantic lifestyle and be a dedicated homemaker. These individuals must be properly matched to those individuals born under Birth Code 5, 8 or 1. You are a very cooperative person and will work easily with others. If you are a woman, you are extremely romantic in your love life and very emotional when it comes to being deceived by others. You are very self-sacrificing and can be an ideal spouse. You love the world and would like to give a lot of yourself to the world.

In your career you may become very popular and well known by your community. You are a good cook and will enjoy others in this way. You are advised not to let your ego dominate your personality as this may create great conflicts in your life. Always try to be humble and spiritual. Usually if you are spiritual, all your wishes are granted in life. You do not wish to be extremely rich but you do require a comfortable lifestyle. Hindus, who are suffering marriage problems, should attend meditation classes, learn how to be humble and pay respects to elders and priests in their community. For prosperity in life, you should always offer something to drink or eat to any person visiting your home. Christians should humble themselves and be more charitable to the church and the community to ward off any negative influences.

Your Life Based on Vedic Birth Code #3
Life According to Vishnu

You are usually very skinny and small in stature with a thin waist.

You are very argumentative and usually think you are right.

You may experience loss of children or abortions in your life.

If woman, you may experience problems with your uterus.

You may also experience cramps or lower back pain.

You are childish in your ways...people think you are immature.

You hesitate to accept responsibility.

You may have many children.

You may be involved in publishing, writing or selling books.

Your career may involve some form of communication.

Threes are creative and disciplined people, associated with the planet Jupiter. Growth, success, luck, happiness and fertility are suggested, though on the negative side the person may also be gossipy, moody, overcritical, sometimes rather shy or pessimistic or unimaginative and prone to leaving jobs half done. You will fare especially well with other 3s.

Karmic Characteristics of Vedic Birth Code #3

Usually you are a very jovial and happy person. In most cases your ego will not allow others to upset you or prevent you from achieving your desires or your satisfaction to be right always. You are very youthful looking and even in old age will look 10 years younger than you really are. You may have a petite body and enjoy such hobbies as dancing, music and swimming. You express yourself very clearly to others and may be asked to give speeches to groups of people. You love children and would very much like to have them around you. Children enjoy your company because you are very playful. Other adults may find you immature at times and in love relationships your partner may think you are very childish in your ways.

If you are negative you may be denied the opportunity of having children. If such is the case, an astrologer may be very helpful to you. You like to read a great deal and can be a good communicator. You may spend a great deal of your time on the phone.

A career associated with electronic communication may be very beneficial to you. Those who are educated may find themselves wanting to publish or write books as you make an excellent author. If you are not religious, your negativity may present you with many difficulties in life that may create great losses through younger people. Also you may experience the sickness of children around you. Christians are advised to meditate on Jesus Christ as a teacher and on the words "The Lord is my shepherd and I am the sheep."

Your Life Based on Vedic Birth Code #4
Life According to Ganesh

You are very hardworking and conscientious.

You have a high temper and may experience many stressful moments.

You are very determined in your attitude and will not admit defeat easily.

If you want something, you are determined to have it at any cost.

Your health may be affected by too much work.

You will do very well in life if you own a home.

Real estate investments are very lucky for you.

There is completeness in 4, because mathematically it is a square. It is associated with the Earth and its 4 seasons, and people under its influence tend to be very down to Earth, systematic, practical and stable, upholding law and order, and using logic and reason in their actions. Yet there is also an earthbound and unimaginative side to these people, who may be over-fussy about small details, lazy, weak and prone to worrying too

42

much. Occasionally, a 4 will have a stubborn, rebellious streak. Friendship is difficult.

Karmic Characteristics of Vedic Birth Code #4

You are an extremely hard-working person and sometimes people refer to you as a workaholic. You are very slow and methodical in your actions. It is very hard for someone to get you to change your mind once you have made a decision. And even if you do agree to comply you may experience difficulty adapting to the change or anything new in life. You are very dutiful in your home and may be found to be constantly doing something around the house.

You make an excellent carpenter and may be very successful in the field of construction. As a contractor you may become very wealthy in life. You are a collector of antiques or articles of memory. You may be the owner of many homes or none if you are negative. You may also be a landlord and if you are negative may experience many troubles and court problems with tenants. You may acquire properties through inheritance from your parents or a dead relative. If you are employed in a business of your own you may be working more hours than you really get compensated for. If you are in a regular job, you may be asked to put in a lot of overtime.

If you are negative, your most major problems in life may be related to your career. Laziness may definitely bring you down to poverty and ruin. You are advised to avoid placing yourself under too much pressure or tension as this may create high blood pressure problems. Avoid overwork and lifting heavy equipment. If you are not an attorney you may experience delays and problems through attorneys. You may experience rheumatic pains in your joints.

If you are a positive person, you may settle down into a very comfortable and large home, well decorated and taken care of by your spouse. Christians are advised to study the experiences of Abraham in the Old Testament.

Your Life Based on Vedic Birth Code #5
Life According to Narayan
You change your mind a great deal and very quickly.
You love to travel and will experience many changes of residence.
It is very hard for others to access your thinking.
You have great intuitive powers and will usually know things ahead of time.
You can read another's personality very easily.
You can feel the energy of others and may know their thoughts about you.
Usually you are too helpful to others to the detriment of yourself...you give too much of yourself.
You do many things to help others without asking for compensation.
Your connection with the Universe is very profound and your mission in life seems to be to help others.
You give great counseling and advice to friends and family.
You are not very lucky with relative and family members.
You make friends easily...friends help you the most in life.
The more good actions in life, the more beneficial it will be for you.
You have the ability to develop psychic powers and heal others by touching.
You may experience problems with the government, IRS or immigration.
At some point in your life you will be influenced greatly by a spiritual leader.

Five represents the senses. There is activity, change, hatred of routine, need for novelty and a reputation for unpredictability. These people are energetic, adaptable, resourceful, intelligent and quick to learn. They may demand too much of others, be too impulsive, and spread themselves too thin with too many projects at once. They make friends very easily, but are difficult to live with.

Karmic Characteristics of Vedic Birth Code #5

Sex, romance, lust, beauty and physical satisfaction are some of the qualities in your life. You are very much attracted to the opposite sex and you, yourself, may be quite a handsome or beautiful person. You may be easily tempted into having illicit affairs if your willpower is weak. On the other hand individuals like you can become the perfect husband or wife. If you find the right spouse you will be extremely faithful. The right spouse in this case means that he or she must be romantic and an extremely willing and skilled lover. If these qualities are present in your marriage everything else falls into place.

You will enjoy traveling and may visit many places in your life. You can bring change to a lot of people's lives and are sometimes great advisers to others but not to yourself. Wherever you are present some change may occur. It is also possible that with proper knowledge and guidance you may bring about enormous changes to world philosophy and thinking. You are a great writer and can tell convincing short stories that may change people's beliefs. It is also possible that you may change your residence many times in your life and may live mostly away from your birthplace.

Your greatest downfall can be lust or sexual indulgences. If you are negative you may want to make love to every member of the opposite sex you come into contact with. Your taste for music can be of a wide variety and you may be concerned mostly with satisfying your bodily needs rather than your mental needs. If you are positive, you may become and extremely skilled businessman or politician and may achieve very wealthy and successful positions in life. At some point in your life you may be accused falsely by others and may be stuck with many debts and loans with you may not be able to repay. You are the carrier of good news or bad news and may even like to gossip or involve yourself in informative conversations. To enjoy this karma you must learn to be sincere in all your actions. Be religious and be respectful to elders and keep an open mind.

Your Life Based on Vedic Birth Code #6
Life According to Kali

You like to be in charge and have a very strong ego.

You may experience a career with many responsibilities, which you may handle well.

If you fail to handle your responsibilities in life you will experience misery.

You may experience lower or upper back pain...if not, headaches or migraines.

A bad diet may affect your blood pressure and health.

If you are not working for the government, you may be constantly harassed due to problems with the government.

If you are having a difficult time repaying your debts, you could lose your home through foreclosure.

You may be very responsible and have a business of your own.

You do not accept astrology or occult studies very easily.

You feel very frustrated, especially when you cannot have things your way.

Your key to happiness is acceptance and spirituality.

You should avoid the color red; it creates pain.

Six is the number of the emotions. Mathematically, 6 is a "perfect number" because it is the sum of its factors,

1, 2, and 3. People under its sway tend to be reliable and well rounded. There is love of home, peace, beauty, and harmony. Sixes tend to be artistic and good with children and animals. They may also be too sympathetic, too self-sacrificing, too stubborn, too concerned with duty, perhaps too interfering. But they are among the most popular of people, making good friends and partners.

Karmic Characteristics of Vedic Birth Code #6

Responsibility, high tempers and power are some of the qualities in your life. It is possible that as a young person growing up you possessed a very strong personality and a high temper. You may have many quarrels with relatives and friends because of jealousy or a battle for power. You like to be in charge and are not willing to take orders from others very easily. You prefer to be a supervisor or boss instead of an employee. Your ego is very high and this may present many difficulties in your life where you may be unable to admit that you are wrong even when you know you are.

If you are negative, it is quite possible that you may suffer from serious pain in your lower back for which doctors are unable to find a cure. You should see the Hindu priest or astrologer for proper advice on how to get rid of this back pain, which can be very irritating sometimes. In addition to this affliction you may also suffer migraine headaches, which may result from your inability to control your inner anger.

If positive and religious, you can make out to be an excellent marriage partner provided you assume proper responsibility for your family and relationships. You are accident-prone and must be careful when handling machinery or vehicles. Employment with the government or the military forces may be very beneficial to you and you are advised to seek such opportunities. On the other hand, you enjoy power and dominion over your life and your environment.

As a leader or supervisor you perform excellently and earn respect from others. If you allow your ego to make you a non-believer in religion or god, you may suffer prolonged diseases such as high blood pressure, heart problems or cancer. These diseases may develop as a result of constantly eating meat, drinking alcohol or taking unnecessary drugs. It is advisable for you to be vegetarian if possible and maintain a meditation schedule. For other non-believers it is possible that you may experience many difficulties with the courts, attorneys and mortgage companies. You must learn to maintain your responsibility with regard to loans or any monies borrowed.

Married individuals may experience many separations from their spouses, possibly as a result of unexpected responsibilities, which may create misunderstandings. People, who are usually divorced as a result of this, may find themselves very unhappy after the divorce for their wealth and prosperity lies in staying married. Christians are advised to read the book of Proverbs and follow the advice given there for worship of the Lord.

Your Life Based on Vedic Birth Code #7
Life According to Shiva
Your mind is running at a thousand miles an hour.
You are constantly thinking and analyzing everything.
Sometimes you keep most of your thoughts to yourself.
You do not tell your plans very easily to others.
You feel you are right in everything 99% of the time.
Sometimes you think everyone is against you.
If woman, you are very beautiful or, if male, handsome.
You attract the opposite sex very easily.
Your need for love and romance is very high.
You experience many difficulties in your marriage.
A sure key to happiness for you is meditation and music.
You are kind hearted and can be deceived easily by your
    lovers.
You should avoid the color black; wear light colors.

Seven is the most significant and magical of the numbers. It has long been held sacred, as is shown by the extraordinary frequency of 7 in mythology, the Bible, and classifications of all kinds. There are 7 notes in the musical scale, 7 phases of the Moon, 7 seas, 7 heavenly bodies in the old Ptolemaic system, 7 wonders of the ancient world, 7 hills of Rome, 7 virtues, 7 deadly sins, 7 days of creation, 7 plagues of Egypt, 7 sentences in the Lord's Prayer, 7 trumpets in the Apocalypse, and many more. The 7th son of a 7th son is believed to possess great magical powers.

People who are 7s are sometimes great thinkers and may have an occult or psychic side. They may be researchers, investigators or inventors. They have an affinity with the sea and often travel widely. But they must use their powers wisely, avoiding pride and cynicism and accepting that their talents will never make them materially rich.

Karmic Characteristics of Vedic Birth Code #7

You have a very secretive and sometimes very private personality. You hardly speak what you are thinking but your mind is running at 100 miles per hour. However, when you do speak, your words are like fire ready to destroy the person you are speaking to. People around you see you as an eggshell ready to break with the slightest intimidation, so your partner or lover feels like he or she is always walking on eggshells because he or she never knows when you are going to find something wrong with him or her. Your criticism of others can be very high and may prevent others from getting very close to you. You tend to hold back a lot of your personal feelings for others. Even your beloved will ask you when are you going to say, "I love you"? It is very important that you do not analyze others too much for no one is perfect in everything. The first lesson you must learn in life is that no one can be perfect. Once you have learned this, your love life and your marriage life will be much happier.

You possess a very high temper and may sometimes speak very harshly to others. If this quality is carried into your marriage it may end in divorce. Out of all others in this astrological analysis you possess the highest ego there is. You will never admit when you are wrong. You will never admit when you feel weak inside, and you will always put up an outward appearance much different from the inner one. Your true feelings never seem to come out, even though your true feelings given to the other person would solve all the problems.

If you are an extremely negative individual, you may be addicted to drugs, alcohol or smoking. You may also be constantly complaining over petty or unnecessary matters. A small matter may worry you a great deal. You are constantly studying or reading if you are not sleeping or relaxing watching TV. You are very slow in your movements and may experience many delays in your life as a result of this.

You may get married very late in life. If you do get married early there may be a possibility of separation. Late marriages are usually more successful. Your interests may lie in the field of medicine, and if you study medical sciences you will be successful in a career associated with it. If you are a positive individual you may become a priest, a yogi or saint. If you are religious you may experience inner encounters with God and other divine manifestations of the universal deities. If you happen to find yourself a guru, you may experience a divine connection through that personality. If this path is followed, most of your wishes will be fulfilled in life and your desires may become a reality. You may encounter many religious individuals in your life. You are advised to pay much attention to what they say for their advice may be very beneficial to you. Respect must be given to all holy people or elders in the family.

Christians are advised to say the Lord's Prayer 11 times every day.

Your Life Based on Vedic Birth Code #8
Life According to Laxmi

You love money and constantly think about it.
You may have a business of your own.
Money flows through your hands very easily.
If you are spiritual and conservative, money will stay.
You love expensive things and may shop a lot.
Your favorite color may be pink if you are female.
You have a strong ego.
Investment in stocks may prove profitable.
You love jewelry and may own of lot of it.
Avoid wearing anything black, as it will kill your prosperity.
Silver and pearl are very lucky for you and will make you prosperous.

These people will achieve success but not necessarily happiness. They may possess the drive and ability to lead, and thus receive material wealth and recognition, but they can often drive themselves too hard, repressing their feelings, suffering tension, and missing out on satisfying relationships.

Karmic Characteristics of Vedic Birth Code #8

All of your actions and your thoughts are related to money. You may become a wealthy businessperson or a bankrupt millionaire. You like to buy expensive and extravagant items. Your taste is very luxurious and your thinking is very materialistic. You worry a great deal about money and may be a big spender or a big saver according to your karma in this life. You may experience sudden prosperity in life and then all of a sudden find yourself in poverty again, for this is a very karmic influence that you are born under. The life that you lead now may account for all the good or bad actions you have performed in previous lives. This is called the judgment life for you. As a businessperson you may own a very large and profitable company. As an employee you may be earning a very high salary.

If you are negative you may be unable to save any money in the bank. You may also experience a great deal of financial problems and may lose money through the opposite sex. Your spending may be more than your income. Other negatives are revolution, rupture, excess materialism, deceit and trickery with regard to money and so on.

On the other hand, if you are a positive and a very spiritual person you could become very powerful and very wealthy. Your understanding of material aspects will be excellent throughout your life and you will be a very successful money earner. You are an excellent negotiator in business transactions and may achieve most of your wealth after your marriage. You possess a special ability to analyze financial trends and gambling secrets that few people may know about. If you are careful about your health and the kind of food you eat, you may live a very long life, possibly up to 108 years. You may become very wealthy through investments in real estate or stock markets.

Your sexual vitality is very high and this may present some interesting romantic adventures in your life. You seek occupations that are very political and powerful such as city manager, corporate director, etc. This power or money could well go the other way as much as its promises can be destructive. This karma is called the judgment of life where all actions from past lives are in this life are accounted for. Christians are advised to follow the parables outlined in the New Testament in the teachings of Christ and look upon him as the true Teacher of mankind.

Your Life Based on Vedic Birth Code #9
Life According to Indra

You may have a high temper and a suspicious mind.

You may experience the death of very close family members.

Take care to avoid accidents and traffic violations.

Alcohol is very damaging to your life; avoid it.

You think very deeply about life and may be extremely religious.

If you are positive you may become famous.

You make a great politician or spiritual guru.

You will live a long life and may work in a hospital.

Working for the government greatly benefits you.

You seem to be always struggling to fulfill your desires in life.

You spend more than you earn and will have financial problems.

You are very honest and may lose in partnerships because of this.

Negative husbands may abuse their wives physically and mentally.

You have a loud voice and love to shout at other sometimes.

The keys to your happiness are to attend churches and donate your time and energy to charitable organizations.

If the #1 symbolizes the beginning, the number #9 embraces all the previous numbers and symbolizes finality and completeness. Numerologically it reproduces itself, as the digits of all multiples of 9 add up to 9; for example, 4x9=36, then 3+6=9. It is a sacred and mystical number with many Biblical and legendary references: 9 orders of angels, a 9 days' wonder, 9 points of the law, 9 months of pregnancy, 9 lives of a cat, and so on.

Nines are determined fighters; they tend to be compassionate, determined, seekers after perfection, but also self-regarding, impulsive, possessive and moody. Their friendships tend to be with 3s and 6s. Sometimes you doubt the existence of God and sometimes you believe in God. You are a child of the sea and must pray to the ocean for the fulfillment of your desires.

Karmic Characteristics of Vedic Birth Code #9

Your temper, your passions and your inner self are constantly erupting like a volcano. If you are positive you may experience a highly spiritual or psychic connection with the Universe. You could become very famous in life and will make an excellent priest or Brahmin. A positive involvement with the government may put you in the position of a police officer, congressman or even president of a country. A negative involvement with the government may bring you into association with criminals, accusation of a crime or in conflict with the courts, the IRS or lawyers.

You are very high natured and usually need the companion of the opposite sex constantly. After marriage your frustrations can easily result in aggressiveness if you are denied sexual attention from your lover. Even though you are aware that you are wrong in many things, you may deny that such things are happening to you and this usually results in negative attractions to life.

If you are negative, you may become an alcoholic or a drug addict. This type of life may surely bring you into contact with the courts and the prisons. Your harshness to others and your temper must be controlled; otherwise you may experience divorces, violent encounters with your spouse or lover and possible exposure to distress from criminals.

On the other hand, if you are positive you may experience many unique religious psychic and astrological experiences. You could become very famous or notorious. It is possible that you may experience misfortune and accidents in the middle part of your life. If you are negative and insult or criticize religious groups or individuals, you may receive a curse from God. This may come in the form of cancer, AIDS, tuberculosis or any other incurable diseases. Your karma in this life is to read, learn, meditate, teach and learn the wisdom of life. Some of you may become hermits, yogis and gurus prepared to save the world from sin and destruction. Your knowledge is very high and encompassing. You could develop a great love for others without boundaries. You usually experience the death of many friends and family. Your home may also be located close to a cemetery or a large body of water. You may also experience natural disasters such as hurricanes and earthquakes, etc.

Your life may change every nine years and, depending upon whether it is positive or negative, the change may follow accordingly. You have the ability to request from god directly all the things you desire in life. However this can be done only if you maintain positive relationship with the government, peaceful love life with your spouse and respectful humility with elders and priests. Even if you are a judge and you have violated the divine principles of life, you may be struck down. The only way to achieve success in your life is to meditate, seek out a teacher and maintain a strict meatless diet. You must always be ready to follow the philosophy of truth and be willing to teach or give without selfishness. Christians are advised to fast and regularly attend church services and do charitable work.

Chapter 8

Your Life Path Based on Your Life Code

The Life Code – Your Purpose Here on Earth

Your Life Code is determined by your Year of Birth. Add the numbers of your birth year in single digits, and the final number will become your Life Code. For example, if you were born in 1956, then your Vedic Life Code is 1+9+5+6=21 or 2+1=3, which is considered to be Vishnu or Moses. The Life Codes are interpreted and explained under the Chapter entitled "Vedic Life Codes."

The purpose of your life and reason for being born is contained in the Vedic Life Code. It determines your path in life, why you are here and what your objectives are in life. If you think of the word "path" it really means "road". If you're really think about it, the road is a pathway usually bordered by fences and or a water canal or conduit. You can drive only on the road and follow the signs; you cannot exit whenever you feel like it. If you do, you could end up in the canal or crash into the fence. Only when the signs guide you to an exit, can you turn off the road. Well, the Life Code acts like road signs, telling you when to turn and when not to turn, or when to exit or when not to exit, technically speaking. The Life Code can make you understand your objectives and goals in a better way that will make you perform your tasks with much more efficiency.

Consult the Table of Year Codes to determine your Life Code. Just add your Birth Code to the code indicated on the following table next to the year of birth and resultant single number will be your Life Code. For example, if you were born in the year 1990, your Birth Year Code will be 1, and when this is added to your Birth Code, let's say Birth Code 2, the result is Life Code #3. Then you will read the interpretation for Life Code #3 that follows the Table of Year Codes.

TABLE 8:1 BIRTH YEAR LIFE CODES									
1901	2	1933	7	1965	3	1997	8	2029	4
1902	3	1934	8	1966	4	1998	9	2030	5
1903	4	1935	9	1967	5	1999	1	2031	6
1904	5	1936	1	1968	6	2000	2	2032	7
1905	6	1937	2	1969	7	2001	3	2033	8
1906	7	1938	3	1970	8	2002	4	2034	9
1907	8	1939	4	1971	9	2003	5	2035	1
1908	9	1940	5	1972	1	2004	6	2036	2
1909	1	1941	6	1973	2	2005	7	2037	3
1910	2	1942	7	1974	3	2006	8	2038	4
1911	3	1943	8	1975	4	2007	9	2039	5
1912	4	1944	9	1976	5	2008	1	2040	6
1913	5	1945	1	1977	6	2009	2	2041	7
1914	6	1946	2	1978	7	2010	3	2042	8
1915	7	1947	3	1979	8	2011	4	2043	9
1916	8	1948	4	1980	9	2012	5	2044	1
1917	9	1949	5	1981	1	2013	6	2045	2
1918	1	1950	6	1982	2	2014	7	2046	3
1919	2	1951	7	1983	3	2015	8	2047	4
1920	3	1952	8	1984	4	2016	9	2048	5
1921	4	1953	9	1985	5	2017	1	2049	6
1922	5	1954	1	1986	6	2018	2	2050	7
1923	6	1955	2	1987	7	2019	3	2051	8
1924	7	1956	3	1988	8	2020	4	2052	9
1925	8	1957	4	1989	9	2021	5	2053	1
1926	9	1958	5	1990	1	2022	6	2054	2
1927	1	1959	6	1991	2	2023	7	2055	3
1928	2	1960	7	1992	3	2024	8	2056	4
1929	3	1961	8	1993	4	2025	9	2057	5
1930	4	1962	9	1994	5	2026	1	2058	6
1931	5	1963	1	1995	6	2027	2	2059	7
1932	6	1964	2	1996	7	2028	3	2060	8
1933	7	1965	3	1997	8	2029	4	2061	9

After finding your Life Code on the Table 8.1, read the following Life Path Code interpretation that corresponds to your Life Path Code.

Your Purpose in Life Based on Life Code #1
When born under this Life Code and following a negative path, you must learn to fall back on your own resources (i.e. your strength and your knowledge) and make your own decisions. You must work on your inner self – mind, body and spirit. You must learn to be original and to establish new ideas, new ideals and new tactics. Try to break away from the standard trends and be your own person.

Perhaps the most important lesson for you to learn is that there are other people in the world besides you. You must learn to live with others without bullying or imposing unjustly your own will power upon them. If you follow a positive path, you will find your way open for positive action and achievement.

Individual action, originality, new creations, progress and ambition are some dominant things in your life. You will possess self-confidence, assurance and pride; your life will be filled with activity. This Life Code indicates that you will usually be able to stand on your own feet and have the desire to be your own person as opposed to being involved with associates or partners.

Learn to be independent. Do not take advantage of others. Be a leader. Be spiritual. Enjoy being alone. Take time to meditate.

Your Purpose in Life Based on Life Code #2
When born under this Life Code and following a negative path, the keyword is subservience. The lesson that you must learn is not to put yourself before others. You must learn cooperation, patience and consideration for others. Learn to overcome shyness and over-sensitivity. When following a positive path, you will find a life full of

cooperation, the ability to work well with others and to follow instructions.

This will be a life full of gentle love and peace, for the karma of this Life Code is to give and to seek love and companionship. Your best role is peacemaker but be aware because unscrupulous people can take advantage of the kindness of people in this form.

Be cooperative. Avoid being too kind. Marry only once. Avoid divorce. Don't be too materialistic. Take care with your words, and do not be too outspoken to others.

Your Purpose in Life Based on Life Code #3

When born under this Life Code and following a negative path, the lesson you must learn is self-expression, to give freely of the self and to share your feelings openly, without fear. One of the biggest dangers you must overcome is that of jealousy. When following the positive path, consider yourself fortunate, for this is the nicest of all codes to have.

This is the code of self-expression in the way of peaceful, enjoyable activities surrounded by beauty, inner peace and harmonious atmosphere. This code will lead to many friends and companions. It will be a life of inspiration, talent and kindness.

Read and write a lot. Avoid childlessness. Accept all responsibilities in life. Avoid abortions and laziness. Learn to bow to all people of authority.

Your Purpose in Life Based on Life Code #4

When born with this Life Code and following a negative path, you must be able to use your ability to apply yourself to detail work. You must learn to stay put, become the cornerstone and devote yourself in duty to your family community and country. A particular danger to overcome is that of unjust hatred. You must learn to cooperate with your spouse, as every little thing that happens to people born under this form can irritate them easily.

When following a positive path, you might still find it a difficult code to live under, as it predicts a life of hard work and effort. The outstanding qualities of this code are the abilities of organization, devotion, dignity, trust and loyalty. Under this code, you will find great responsibility because of your outstanding qualities and will confer a wide range of trust, many times unwanted.

Work hard. Listen to your employers. Avoid stress. Save your money. Avoid gambling, investments, and shady (unclear) deals. Do not be too harsh in your judgment of others.

Your Purpose in Life Based on Life Code #5

If you were born under this Life Code and are following a negative path, your keyword is freedom. You must learn to change your thoughtlessness and be ready to accept frequent, unwanted changes. Drinking habits, narcotics, sensuality and sex can be deadly if overindulged.

If following a positive path, you might still find this Life Code to be a difficult but varied one to live under. You will experience frequent changes in all aspects of your life in which there will be much variety and travel. You will have freedom, curiosity, adventure, aloneness and progress. Above all, your life will be the center of constant change.

Watch your back. Avoid secret love affairs. Traveling is a must. Be careful whom you trust. Help others willingly. Do not be too narrow- minded. Listen to others.

Your Purpose in Life Based on Life Code #6

If born under this Life Code and following a positive path, you will find that it leads to glory and greatness. Many people born under this code have been held back from their destinies because of negative aspects. The greatest problem you face is adjusting to circumstances and accepting things for their true value without looking for perfection in everything. Adjustment is the key word, particularly concerning domestic relationships. You must develop a willingness to serve family, friends and country. You must learn to serve without using tyranny.

If following a positive path, you may realize a quick assent to power and greatness in the material, military or political worlds. It will be a life of responsibility and service and very much the path of adjustments.

If you follow this path, you will be called upon time and time again to settle disputes, make adjustments and render final decisions. Avoid disobeying government laws and follow all traffic rules, for trouble with the police is predicted. The couple whose lives involve this Life Code must avoid encouraging family visitors and involvement with family affairs.

Family interference is your karma. Avoid conflicts. Be responsible. Control your anger and ego. Obey rules. Learn to follow advice of older people. Realize there are laws that need to be followed. Family is your test.

Your Purpose in Life Based on Life Code #7

If born under this form and following a negative path, you will create coldness towards others. You must also overcome aloofness, which results from daydreaming and mentally wandering off, for this can prevent you from performing your responsibilities. You are humiliated and embarrassed easily or embarrass others and are faithless, which can lead to disbelief in God. You must learn to go though life cheerfully accepting the problems and troubles of others.

If following a positive path, you will find this form to be that of the loner, especially with matters concerning the inner self. This is the Life Code of the philosopher, the deep thinker and dreamer. In this code you will find peace, spirituality, trust, faith, research and wisdom. Your life will be restful and peaceful and will not be too concerned with material things.

Learn to be independent. Don't take advantage of others. Be a leader. Be spiritual. Enjoy being alone. Learn to express your feelings openly. Do not hold back emotions. Develop your speech.

Your Purpose in Life Based on Life Code #8

If born under this Life Code and following a negative path, your key word is avoidance of greediness, jealousy and overspending. You will find that you possess a love of power and money, and power for self, intolerance, abuse and revenge. The need is to cultivate [grow] good moral business ethics and understanding of people with less force and dynamics.

If following a positive path, then this will lead you to power, authority, material and financial gains and success in all material aspects. Persons born under this form will be generous and dependable. There is outstanding inner strength and courage.

Control greed for money. Be content. Respect your mother. Control your need for luxury. Be humble. Your ego is too strong for others sometimes. Control your desire for expensive things.

Your Purpose in Life Based on Life Code #9

If you were born under this Life Code and are following a negative path, you will find the need to hold emotions in balance and your self-ego in check. A few of the pitfalls are fickleness, immortality and daydreaming. Once again, if negative, there is a possibility that you could end up in court or become a criminal. You must learn to avoid constant ego quarrels between couples and older family members and to not interfere in other's lives.

If following a positive path, then being born under this code is the all-encompassing destiny. You likely will be a world traveler and have a global outlook. You will be understanding, intuitive, knowledgeable and willing to sacrifice. You usually make marriage partners and lovers and are full of kindness and consideration. It is predicted that you would do well with a career in government agencies.

Health is your karma and it can decline if you are too suspicious, controlling and/or commanding. Believe in God at all times (not sometimes). Control your spending habits. Pay your bills first before anything else.

Chapter 9

The Vedic Hereditary Code

An apple comes from an apple tree. Any fruit can carry only the ingredients of the tree from whence it came. At the time of pregnancy, all that took life from the parents during the nine months of gestation, whatever experiences and emotions took place in the life of the parents, have inculcated into the unborn baby.

Think about this carefully. If a woman is treated cruelly and abused during the nine months of pregnancy, wouldn't the unborn baby absorb all the negative emotions she expressed while being ill-treated? Imagine if a pregnant woman was pampered with lots of love and attention during the period of pregnancy. How do you think the unborn baby would be affected?

In genetic science, we know that the physical traits of parents such as the nose, eyes, etc. are transferred to the unborn child as gestation takes place. Are you aware also that besides physical traits, the spiritual traits of the parents are also transferred to the unborn child? Just as the egg and sperm of the parents is unseen by the naked eye, so also the unseen karma of the parents is transferred to the child during pregnancy. These karmic characteristics take hold of your life from birth to death. These inherited karmic characteristics affect your behavior, responses, feelings and emotions with others throughout your life.

If we are aware of what our parents were doing at the time of the pregnancy, we could use this information to determine the weaknesses and strengths in our inherited karma. We could then be able to live a more successful life using this information to improve on our weaknesses and cash in on our strengths. For example, if a person has Vedic Birth Code #2, this would indicate that this person, mother or father, at the time of pregnancy, yearned for attention during the pregnancy. The child, after he or she was born, would want to hug and embrace a great deal in life. They would have a problem saying no to people because of their soft-heartedness.

In the following paragraphs, under each Vedic Hereditary Code, we describe the experiences and events that happened in your parents' lives at the time of the pregnancy; they became your inheritance. Using your Vedic Birth Code from Chapter 6, check your Vedic Hereditary Code below.

Vedic Hereditary Code #1
Your life may become lonely.
You could become a widow or widower.
You will have to become independent and do things for
    yourself.
Your path is that of a leader and creator of things.
With your creative ability you should invent things.
Too many illicit affairs could make you suffer
    disabilities.

Vedic Hereditary Code #2
You must lead a life of love, cooperation, embraces and
    willingness to do things for others.
Marriage will be happy and comfortable.
You will be a good cook, restaurant chef or hostess.
Love & service to others will be your test in life.
Being too outspoken could hurt those you love.
Speak your heartfelt feelings with forethought.

Vedic Hereditary Code #3
You will look younger than you are always.
Childish in your ways, you like attention and will
    throw a tantrum if you do not get attention
    especially from partners.

You will benefit greatly from reading, writing, teaching, babysitting or pediatrics.

You like to listen to stories and you make a good storyteller; avoid gossiping.

Vedic Hereditary Code #4

You will have to work very hard for your money and to achieve position in your career.

Laziness and idleness will destroy your life.

You will gain weight if you are lazy and do not exercise.

You will suffer from high blood pressure and stress unless you learn to relax and eat properly after doing your tasks.

Vedic Hereditary Code #5

You always want to believe only what you think is right.

You always want to gain and win in anything you do for others.

You have very sensitive skin and can experience psoriasis or skin cancer.

You will suffer from some kind of foot problems.

You will have difficulty in married life if your partner is not willing to bow to you and serve you.

Sex and sexuality will be your test in life; you admire the physical forms of the opposite sex.

Vedic Hereditary Code #6

You have a fear of separation from family and lovers.

You get frustrated quickly which leads to anger sometimes.

You will love power, high status and prestige in life.

You can be unlucky with government if you are negative.

You are a beacon to the police; you may have many traffic tickets.

Responsibility is your test in this life – accept all tasks given.

Vedic Hereditary Code #7

You suppress your feelings so as to avoid conflicts with others.

Your mind is constantly analyzing and rechecking things.

Your love life is your greatest test since you do not express love.

You could become highly religious or an alcoholic or drug addict.

You would make a good radio announcer or news/talk show anchor.

You have to be careful of overindulgence and excesses.

You could be psychic or part of a mission in life.

Vedic Hereditary Code #8

Money, comfort and wealth are your most important priorities in this life.

Much money will pass through your hands; control your spending.

You like fashions and may wish to become a model or an actor.

You like expensive things and a socially extravagant life.

You may find yourself exchanging sexual favors for money.

You could have a business or sales position in a large corporation.

If you are poor, you inherited this curse from you parents.

Vedic Hereditary Code #9

You will experience sickness, death or separation in childhood.

You will struggle very hard to meet your goals in life.

You will constantly go through denial about your life and God.

You could experience court cases, imprisonment or accidents.

You could become very famous, highly religious or
notorious.

Being spiritual and praying to the sea gods will help
you in life.

Money spends very easily in your hands; try hard to
save.

As soon as you save a large amount, you get the urge
to spend it.

Avoid lending others money and impulsive buying
habits.

Chapter 10

The Childbirth Code
Lucky or Unlucky Birthdays

Why are some birthdays lucky or unlucky?
As we have stated before, you are the fruit of your parents; they are the tree. Whatever the condition of the tree at the time of the fruit bearing, so will be the fruit. Similarly whenever a woman is pregnant, her feelings, experiences and conditions at the time of pregnancy will determine the Karmic Birth Code of the baby.

When a child is born at an inauspicious time, at that moment for that day, the Vedic degree of the Moon will be important in determining whether the time of birth was bad or good. We all know that the Moon controls the tides on Earth as well as the ovulation period of women and their menstrual cycle, as well as blood pressure in all humans. Using the Moon degree to determine the bad and good days for birth is a more secure system than others are, since the revolution of the Moon in time never is incorrect.

If a child is born in an unfortunate degree of the Moon, then there can be death, sickness, separation and health problems or accidents to specific members of the family. To avoid these effects, the father of the baby should not look at the baby until after 9 days of birth and to bathe at the sea 3 days before seeing the baby's eyes. Another method would be to place a layer of mustard oil on a shiny metal pan and look at the baby's eyes in a reflection prior to actually holding the baby.

For many years, pundits and students of this science have consulted me, asking the reason for some of the disasters that followed the birth of a baby in the family. The knowledge of unfortunate birthdays is an ancient one but apparently was partially lost over the centuries, as our people gave up the transcendental side of life in exchange for the temporary existence of material life. True knowledge gave way to aggressiveness and quest for material acquisitions. Hence people forgot about checking with priests and astrologers about their birthdays.

Ancient scientists knew that when babies were born, it was the coming of the soul with all of its "good" and "bad" karma. All of this energy is concentrated in the eyes and face of the baby. If, however, this energy is negative, it is transferred immediately to the eyes of the father, who will then carry it for awhile as he communicates with family members. Usually this "negative" energy can cause death of the child, separation of its parents, death of a family member or family relation. If the proper Vedic rules are not followed, the baby throughout its life will carry this energy and at the time of marriage it can cause death of the in-laws or other relatives.

Today, fathers are asked to be with the mother in the hospital and watch the birth of the baby. This is dangerous. If a child is born under an unfortunate day, the father should not see the child until the proper remedies are met and done. Under no circumstances should the father look at the eyes of the baby until the remedies are done.

Below you will find the specific Birth Codes in combination with Life Path Codes that apply to the unfortunate birthday effects that require your concern.

TABLE 10:1- BIRTH CODE EFFECTS vs AGE & EFFECT ON LIFE		
VEDIC BIRTH CODES	**VEDIC LIFE CODES**	**EVENTS AND POSSIBLE EFFECTS ON THESE BIRTHS** *Please Note: Final Conclusions should be made after consultion with other Vedic Code Consultants*
9	2	Possible effects on Mother and Government problems
9	1	Possible sickness, accidens and early death of Grandparents
6	2	Possible sickness to self and separation of family members
6	1	Possible sickness to self and separation of family members
9	1	Major sickness from diseases or constant health problems
6	2	Early death or accidents to Family Members
6	6	Possible sickness to self and separation of family members
1	9	Disease and sickness to parents early in life
1	6	Major problems in health and Marraiage and love life
9	9	Financial, Hardships and early death of Family members
6	9	Danger to Uncle, Father and Father's family in health etc.
9	1	Accidents or sickness to father's side of the family

There are other types of unfortunate birthdays that are very important for you to consider when checking the birth of a baby. They are as follows:

1: PREMATURE BIRTHS
❖   5th month - Will affect the love life of the parents
❖   6th month - Will create conflict in family
❖   7th month - Will attract religious enemies
❖   8th month - Will affect parents' finances

The 4th or 13th born child has to work hard for his or her living.

The 6th or 15th born child will suffer tremendously with health problems.

The 9th or 18th born child will suffer from financial government problems.

If a boy is born after 3 girls are born or a girl is born after 3 boys are born, it is considered unlucky.

There are also more serious types of unfortunate births. Some people can be born under the Snake Energy. Usually, this is observed as hairs growing on the back in the shape of a snake from the bottom of the spine to the head. In such case, death of the spouse will be immediate after sexual consummation. Special remedies are available to counteract this effect before marriage. A special tuft of hair in the middle of the back of a person will guarantee the death of an elder person of the in-law side of the family.

Another type of unfortunate birth is evident when a woman or a man has flat feet, i.e.: there is no arch on the bottom of the foot. This affliction causes the person to lose all the money and property of the household in which he or she resides.

Some Case Histories to Illustrate This Vedic Code
In one of my recent experiences, a baby was born in Kritikka Nakshatra. The family consulted with me after enduring one disaster after another. I found out that the grandfather had died two months after the birth. Immediately thereafter, the baby was afflicted with epilepsy. Repeated visits to hospitals and doctors did not help. After I was called, I found out that the family

was suffering from the effects of the baby's unfortunate Birth Code. I gave the proper instructions to the parents but perhaps doubt entered their minds.

They called a local Hindu priest to get a second opinion and he told the parents that he did not think that this was going to be an unfortunate Birth Code. The proper remedies were not followed, due to the parents' doubt. Sad to say, a week later the baby died. The family called me again, and I explained that the baby died because the proper procedures were not followed. I knew that this was not the end of disaster in that family. Other family members were in line for problems. So I made a personal call to the priest in question. Thankfully, he was not blinded by ego, but rather was quite receptive to my teaching. After our discussion, he performed the proper procedures, and the family achieved some peace in their lives thereafter.

Afterword by Swami Ram
I am saddened to see needless suffering in hundreds of families within our community. Our Vedic Code of Science books are so rich with information that they can easily help us all live in happiness and harmony. I urge you to listen to that "small voice" within yourself rather than following blindly any advice that you receive. If you are not sure of or confident in an answer, consult with spiritual advisors. May the Gods bless you with the true knowledge that is enclosed in these chapters! If you cannot find your answers or remedies, please feel free to call the Center for Vedic Science in Miami, Florida.

In the following table, take your Vedic Birth Code (Chapter 6) and find your Vedic Childbirth Code, then read the interpretation for your Vedic Childbirth Code.

TABLE 10:2 - VEDIC CHILDBIRTH CODES								
YOUR DAY OF BIRTH								
YOUR MONTH OF BIRTH	*1* *10* *19* *28*	*2* *11* *20* *29*	*3* *12* *21* *30*	*4* *13* *22* *31*	*5* *14* *23*	*6* *15* *24*	*7* *16* *25*	*8* *17* *26*	*9* *18* *27*
JANUARY	2	3	4	5	6	7	8	9	1
FEBRUARY	3	4	5	6	7	8	9	1	2
MARCH	4	5	6	7	8	9	1	2	3
APRIL	5	6	7	8	9	1	2	3	4
MAY	6	7	8	9	1	2	3	4	5
JUNE	7	8	9	1	2	3	4	5	6
JULY	8	9	1	2	3	4	5	6	7
AUGUST	9	1	2	3	4	5	6	7	8
SEPTEMBER	1	2	3	4	5	6	7	8	9
OCTOBER	2	3	4	5	6	7	8	9	1
NOVEMBER	3	4	5	6	7	8	9	1	2
DECEMBER	4	5	6	7	8	9	1	2	3

A Simple Way to Assess Your Birthday Code Effect for that Day

Look up your birthday and note the code next to it, then check the paragraph that follows to see the effect of your birthday or anyone else's birthday in your family.

Vedic Code Meanings for Lucky and Unlucky Birthdays

If Your Vedic Childbirth Code is #1, Then...

Mother and father were lonely at the time of the pregnancy.
Mother felt that she had to do a lot of chores on her own without help from anyone.
Father was very independent and bossy.

Mother worried a lot about her husband and felt lonely if he didn't come home early.

Father felt independent and didn't like to be questioned by his wife constantly.

Your birthday is 65 percent negative, indicating that at the time of birth, one of your parents was left alone or felt lonely for the period from conception until you were three years old. One of your parents was very occupied with other things, leaving the other to do everything alone. This birthday is not unlucky for the parents but will present some bad obstacles in love life and career positions for you.

If Your Vedic Childbirth Code is #2, Then...
Mom wanted a lot of attention from Dad during the pregnancy.

Mom was more loving to Dad during pregnancy.

Dad use to hug Mom a lot and she missed his embraces.

Mom was kindhearted to all and had difficulty saying no to anyone when asked for favors.

Dad was very kind hearted and had a lot of friends when she was pregnant with you and invited them to the home a lot.

Mom constantly took care of visitors and cooked a great deal of food for them. She shopped a lot.

Mom liked jewelry, sweet food and getting dressed up.

If Your Vedic Childbirth Code is #3, Then...
Mom and Dad watched a lot of movies on TV and enjoyed going out to see films.

Mom and Dad socialized a great deal and had many parties and friends.

Mom always had a controlling effect on Dad.

If Your Vedic Childbirth Code is #4, Then...
Mom and Dad worked hard during the pregnancy.

Mom and Dad had lots of stress over career.
Mom and Dan experienced low pay and hard work.
Dad had trouble with co-workers at his workplace.
Dad experienced jealousy and competition at the job site.

If Your Vedic Childbirth Code is #5, Then...

Mom did not trust Dad during the pregnancy.
She accused him of not being sincere with her.
Family was not grateful or thankful to Dad and Mom.
One parent was unfaithful and distrusting.

If Your Vedic Childbirth Code is #6, Then...

Mom had problems with the in-laws and family during
    pregnancy.
There were arguments with in-laws and family
    members on both sides.
Mom was frustrated with the family & in-laws.
Mom feared losing family and attention of her husband.
There were threats and the fear of separation between
    couples.
They had police or court problems before or after birth.
Mom and Dad ate lots of meat and struggled for power
    at the job.

If Your Vedic Childbirth Code is #7, Then...

Mom was very critical of Dad during the pregnancy.
Mom was worried about Dad leaving her for someone
    else.
Both Mom and Dad kept their hurtful feelings inside.
Both Mom and Dad listened to a lot of music.
One of them was either religious or addicted to alcohol.
Mom was picky, particularly during her pregnancy.

If Your Vedic Childbirth Code is #8, Then...

Both Mom and Dad were worried about money and
    career.
Dad might have been worried about a raise or promotion.

Either career or business problems occupied their minds.

Mom wanted to be a model or fashion designer or go partying.

Dad was involved in investments of some sort and lost money.

If Your Vedic Childbirth Code is #9, Then...

Suffering, struggles and financial problems occupied the minds of the parents during the pregnancy.

Trouble with in-laws, jealousy and suspicion were present in this pregnancy.

Forced sexual experiences, loss of reputation and quarrels between partners affected the unborn child.

Someone older may have died before or after the pregnancy.

Chapter 11

The Vedic Name Sound Code

The first sound of your name determines your attitude towards others and life in general. Match the first two letters of your first name to the left column below to get your Sound Code.

TABLE 11:1 - VEDIC NAME CODES

MATCH THE FIRST THREE (OR TWO) LETTERS OF YOUR FIRST NAME TO THE LETTER SHOWN BELOW AND CHECK THE NUMBER ON THE RIGHNT - THIS IS YOUR VEDIC NAME CODE

AA	1	DI	4	HA	9	MU	7	QA	9	UQ	2
AB	3	DO	1	HC	2	NA	6	QE	4	US	4
AC	4	DU	7	HE	4	NE	1	QI	8	UT	5
AD	5	EA	6	HI	8	NF	2	QO	5	UU	6
AE	6	EB	7	HO	5	NI	5	QU	2	UV	7
AF	7	EC	8	HQ	7	NO	2	RA	1	UW	8
AG	8	ED	9	HS	9	NU	8	RE	5	UX	9
AH	1	EF	2	HU	2	NY	3	RI	9	UY	1
AI	9	EG	3	HW	4	OA	7	RO	6	UZ	2
AJ	2	EH	4	HY	6	OB	8	RU	3	VA	5
AK	2	EI	5	IA	1	OC	9	SA	2	VE	9
AL	3	EJ	6	IB	2	OD	1	SE	6	VI	4
AM	6	EK	7	IC	3	OE	2	SI	1	VO	1
AN	5	EL	8	ID	4	OF	3	SO	7	VU	7
AO	7	EM	9	IE	5	OG	4	SU	4	WA	6
AP	8	EN	1	IF	6	OH	5	TA	3	WE	1
AQ	1	EO	2	IG	7	OI	6	TB	4	WI	5
AR	9	EP	3	IH	8	OJ	7	TC	5	WO	2
AS	2	EQ	4	IO	6	OK	8	TD	6	WU	8
AT	3	ER	5	IU	3	OL	9	TE	7	XA	7
AU	4	ES	6	JA	2	OM	1	TF	8	XE	2

TABLE 11:1 - VEDIC NAME CODES

MATCH THE FIRST THREE (OR TWO) LETTERS OF YOUR FIRST NAME TO THE LETTER SHOWN BELOW AND CHECK THE NUMBER ON THE RIGHNT - THIS IS YOUR VEDIC NAME CODE

AV	5	ET	7	JE	6	ON	2	TI	2	XI	6
AW	6	EU	8	JI	1	OO	3	TO	8	XO	3
AX	7	EV	9	JO	7	OP	4	TU	5	XU	9
AY	8	EW	1	JU	4	OQ	5	UA	4	XW	2
AZ	9	EX	2	KA	3	OR	6	UB	5	XY	4
BA	3	EY	3	KE	7	OS	7	UC	6	YA	8
BE	7	EZ	4	KI	2	OT	8	UD	7	YE	3
BI	2	FA	7	KO	8	OU	9	UE	8	YI	7
BO	8	FE	2	KU	5	OV	1	UF	9	YO	4
BU	5	FI	6	LA	4	OW	2	UG	1	YU	1
BY	9	FO	3	LE	8	OX	3	UH	2	ZI	8
CA	4	FQ	5	LI	3	OY	4	UI	3	ZO	5
CB	5	FU	9	LO	9	OZ	5	UJ	4	ZU	2
CE	8	GA	8	LU	6	PA	8	UK	5	CH	2
CI	3	GC	1	MA	5	PE	3	UL	6	PR	7
CO	9	GE	3	ME	9	PF	4	UM	7	KH	1
CU	6	GI	7	MI	4	PI	7	UN	8	CH	3
DA	5	GO	4	MJ	5	PO	4	UO	9	SH	9
DE	9	GU	1	MO	1	PU	1	UP	1	MA	5

After obtaining the code for the sound of your name, read below to find out how your name affects you in your attitude towards life.

If Your Vedic Name Sound Code is #1...Then

You are independent, seeking to achieve status and position in your life. You are usually a good leader and great achiever in your career. Usually the first 9 years of life is very trial-some and testing. If the first letter is 'A', you are usually separated from your family for a while before age 6. If 'A' is the second letter, then you separate from your family after age 12 and are given lots of responsibility to handle at this young age. If 'A' follows 'R' then you become very popular in your trade and community. You will be interested in metaphysical subjects, such as astrology, occult sciences and other mystical subjects.

If Your Vedic Name Sound Code is #2...Then

You will be highly respected and loved by many. You are kind to the needy and poor. You are fond of hot drinks. You earn from silk, cotton, fertilizer, hotel or agricultural products. You are a materialistic individual who generally concentrates on the physical side of life. You are usually of highly sexual nature and involve yourself in social pleasures, such as parties, discos, etc. With 'E' as the first or second vowel in your name, you are very handsome or beautiful. You are approached arduously by the opposite sex.

If Your Vedic Name Sound Code is #3...Then

You are usually successful in life and are almost always in a position of comfort and luxury. You also tend to be family oriented and very understanding of their attitudes. You are very intelligent and wise, yet you tend to become lazy or overwhelmed with an overeating habit, which could be damaging. You are always looking for a bargain and are willing to negotiate deals that save money. You are good entertainers and sometimes are popular in your career and community. People whose names begin with letters A, I F, J, S, Y and R will usually be envious of you and may even try to make life difficult for you.

If Your Vedic Name Sound Code is #4...Then

You are a very caring and responsible individual. You could become very wealthy in life. You would make a good doctor or politician. You are a good leader and will always think about the consequences of your actions before you proceed. You study very hard and are usually highly educated, graduating with honors most of the time. You hold a very high status at your place of employment. Very few people take advantage of you, however, you do come into conflict with people whose names begin with A, I, R and Y.

If Your Vedic Name Sound Code is #5...Then

You are a very good looking and beautiful person who loves sex and passion. You also love money, luxury, and expensive and extravagant items in life. You tend to dress immaculately and fashionably. You are always looking for opportunities to enjoy all the pleasures life has to offer. Usually you are not able to stay in one location very long. You tend to move from place to place very frequently and travel a great deal. You do not like to keep permanent relationships. The first thing that comes to your mind when meeting someone is the pleasure you might gain from that person. You usually take advantage of people whose names begin with any letter in the alphabet.

If Your Vedic Name Sound Code is #6...Then

You are a very independent individual who constantly strives to dominate and lead. When in a leadership position you will do very well in life. However, in marriages you encounter a lot of problems because you are sometimes selfish in your feelings. Usually you try to satisfy yourself only and do something for someone only if you will gain from it. When you encounter people whose names begin with G, O, P and W, you usually have conflict and disagreements. When religious, you become very powerful and independent. The same will occur if you are political. You would make a good businessperson or advisor.

If Your Vedic Name Sound Code is #7...Then

Critical and sometimes very judgmental, you should first look at yourself instead of the faults of others. By the law of God, you are required to be spiritual if you wish to live happily in this life. You are very secretive in nature and even though you are attracted to the supernatural or the occult subjects you will not admit it. You are a very private person and will not reveal your affairs or give your trust to others very easily. You favor the medical profession and may try to be a doctor or nurse in a medical institution. You are a deep thinker and will achieve great heights in your educational field. You will make many religious journeys when you are older. During your lifetime you will come into contact with many religious individuals of great stature.

If Your Vedic Name Sound Code is #8...Then

You will be happy in most of your life. You will inherit wealth from your maternal grandfather. You have a good education. You get several opportunities to mingle with learned persons and exchange ideas with them. In employment, you will be lucky to have a good, intelligent and considerate person as your boss. You are a very responsible individual who holds a high-status position in life. In most cases, you will experience a separation from one of your parents before age 9. This is a divine preparation that is intended to make you think independently and prepare you for the wealth and power that will come to you later in life. You are usually a very stubborn individual who is determined to succeed. Failure is disastrous to your personality. You could become very famous later in life.

If Your Vedic Name Sound Code is #9...then

You always strive with difficulty to achieve your objectives and spend most of your life finding yourself or your identity. You are usually very conflicting in your thoughts and emotions and are sometimes caught between your head and your heart. You could become addicted to something negative, such as alcohol, gambling or drugs. Usually, if you are religious, most of these negative qualities go away. You also develop feelings of jealousy very easily and can go to the extreme of destroying yourself as well as your relationships with others. You are very dedicated workers and truthful in your intentions. Once religious, you can get very close to the Supreme Spirit.

Chapter 12

The Location Code

Your Universal Coordinates
Affect the Way You Live

People, who have been on both the Northern and Southern hemispheres, know that the water runs down a drain in counter-clockwise direction south of the equator and clockwise in the Northern Hemisphere.

Hurricanes, tornadoes and other low-pressure storm centers in the Northern Hemisphere swirl in the counter-clockwise motion, but in the Southern Hemisphere this is reversed. Even smoke spirals upward in the opposite direction on each half of the Earth.

If seen from "above" (North), the planets of the solar system appear to rotate in a counter-clockwise motion. From the southern side of the solar system ("below"), they seem to rotate in the opposite direction.

No civilization of any kind has ever originated in the Southern Hemisphere; people from the Northern Hemisphere founded every modern nation existing south of the equator today. This dominance of the north over the south manifests itself even among nations, states, and cities. Wherever a war or conflict has arisen – either civil or international – the northern nation or northern part of that nation emerges victorious or dominant.

Southern Ireland is one example; both before and after the American Civil War, the North dominated the South in this country and it still does. Although Washington, D.C. is the nation's Capital, New York is the financial center of this country (New York being farther north than Washington).

The United States traditionally dominates Mexico, while Mexico, in turn, dominates its neighbors to the south, except for those in the Southern Hemisphere where the situation seems to be reversed. For this reason, South Africa will never be dominated or conquered by any other African nation. Canada, on the other hand, has not yet fully developed its potential. Yet this northern nation has always come out ahead of its dealings with the United States, a much more powerful and industrially developed land. Canada, therefore, is the land of the future, as are other nations in the northernmost climate.

Civilization moves westward on the terrestrial sphere and dominance moves northward. If the borders of two nations occupy the same general latitudes, then the nations whose capital city is farther north will always be somewhat of its neighbor (or rival). Look at China's dominance over India and her rivalry with Russia.

A lot more than severe weather conditions led to the defeat of both France's and Germany's great armies in their invasions of Russia. And why was it that the mighty Soviet Union could not defeat the little country of Finland in the late 1930s?

During a Vedic Ritual, we divide the Universe into smaller and smaller units until we arrive at the specific address at which the Vedic Ritual is being conducted. In this same way, the Earth is divided and sectioned into tiny units, which become our house lot numbers.

Just as each grain of rice that ends up on your dinner plate had your name imprinted on it from the time it grew through the time that it was harvested, hulled, bagged and shipped to your neighborhood store, in that same way, each plot of Earth attracts a particular individual to its location. This attraction is karmic. Just as a #9 person gets a "chance" to be born as a #9, so too do certain plots of Earth get a "chance" to attain the lot #9.

There is a "Cosmic Will" that governs the allocation and each of us end up at that particular location with that particular lot number because of this Divine Will. Like the #9 individual, who is confused about his identity and his relationship to God or to Devil, so too is a #9 location "confused" about its state of calmness or explosiveness. If the householder follows the path of non-violence and attains a high degree of spirituality, the location can be very calm and peaceful. Thus, #9 locations are good for temples or other places of worship.

On the other hand, if the householder follows the sinful and greedy paths, the location will constantly erupt with fights and quarrels from the people who live there. The householder will face financial hardships, difficulty with children, problems with health and a general state of unhappiness with life. This outcome is much more common among householders in #9 locations because #9 locations attract a particular person in order to allow them to experience the suffering and losses that they have to face. In other words, this is their payback for the karmic deeds they had committed some time before.

In this Age of Darkness, people are more prone to be materialistic and seem to be less devoted to God. Thus in many families, there is a preponderance of sinfulness and greedy behaviors and perhaps only small portions of Godly behavior. Once alcoholism, butchering of animals, drugs, violence, rudeness, arrogance and boastfulness become predominant in a #9 location, the family begins to suffer. Job problems, business failures, financial losses, wayward children, sewer problems, house repairs, medical problems, and car accidents are some of the common distress symptoms that will begin to surface. All of this will happen amid frequent quarrels in the home, and life will continue in a state of constant tension and unhappiness. If this goes on for any extended period of time, the family will self-destruct and will finally be forced to sell the property.

Careful observation of the real estate market will reveal that a high percentage of Vedic House Codes #9 and #6 properties go on sale. Often times if the circumstances are known, it can be revealed that the seller is in some form of distress.

Auspicious Parts of the Home
In the following paragraphs we will be looking first at how the different locations within the home are lucky or unlucky. The direction in which the home faces through the front door forms the basis by which a home is judged. As we mentioned above, the eastern direction is always auspicious.

The Entrance
Divide the plot into 9 sections according to the direction of the house as requested below. Usually the 4th section from the left would be the main entrance door of the house. If not, then some remedies should be followed to correct this effect.

For a House Facing East
Divide the plot into 9 sections. These respectively signify, in order, dissatisfaction, weakness, pecuniary gain, royal favor, enormous wealth, physical weakness, abundant happiness, deep grief and intimidation.

For a House Facing South
Divide the plot similarly into 8 sections. These indicate danger to life, bondage, endearment, protection, and a gain of seeds, mental affliction, fear of disease, disability.

For a House Facing North
The 8 sections produce, in order, insult to wife, lack of strength, harm, gain of seeds, monetary gain, increase of prosperity, acquisition of all fortune and disease. The construction of an entry to a house should not be commenced when the wife of the owner is pregnant, as the issue could be disastrous to her.

Here is an example of how to divide the house. This is a diagram of a house facing East.

TABLE 12:1- CHART OF THE AUSPICIOUS PARTS OF THE HOME FOR A HOUSE FACING EAST the divisions are

LEFT	1	2	3	4	5	6	7	8	9	RIGHT
NORTH	Feelings of not being fully satisfied	Feelings of Weakness	Gain of Money	Feeling like a king or queen	PROSPERITY	Weak body and feelings of pain	Blessings of Great wealth	Deep grief and sadness	Fear and feelings of hurt and rejection	SOUTH
				FRONT DOOR		EAST				

Chapter 13

THE VEDIC BUILDING CODE

The General Effect of Location on Its Inhabitants

Add up the digits of the building or home number to get a single digit as the Vedic Building Code. For example, if your house address is 3149 Macabee Drive, add the 3+1+4+9 and then reduce the results (17) to a single digit to get the Vedic Building Code, i.e. 1+7=8. The #8 is the Vedic Building Code for this address. The name of the street is not important. If the address were 3993, the Vedic Building Code would be #6. Now add up your address number on your home (or apartment) and then read the interpretation of your house code below.

Vedic Building Code #1
This home is usually a very large home or in the extreme very small. People who live in this home are achievers and individualistic personalities who are constantly seeking to lead and dominate. This indicates that new ideas are created or new projects are being thought of constantly in this home.

People who are negative in this type of home are usually lonely and tend to seek solitary moments when they are troubled. To avoid any and all troubles, they should welcome all visitors in this home as special guests and always give them something to drink or something to eat. Divine pictures must be placed in the eastern corner of the house.

Vedic Building Code #2
A loving couple sometimes resides in this home. Individuals living here are very cooperative and helpful to each other and to visitors. True love between the residents of this

home exists and children are also well behaved in the home. Usually this home is a medium-sized home and is well decorated by the elder females in the house. Food is cooked always in this home and the inhabitants love to shop and decorate.

To obtain maximum benefits in this location one should be very cooperative, generous and kind to all. A picture of mother or grandmothers should be maintained in the northern corner of this house and, for Christians, a picture of the Virgin Mary should be maintained in the same location.

Vedic Building Code #3

A home with this number consists of all comforts, lots of food and a lot to drink. Some of these homes are extremely large also. A large television or movie rack is definitely a part of this home. The occupants of this home are very youthful looking and there are usually many children living in this home. The absence of children in this home will indicate that unhappiness exists here. A library is also present and people in this home are supposed to read a lot of books.

In this home also many people find it very comfortable to pursue educational studies and the children who live here will definitely attend some college or university. Little angels or child angels govern this house. Pictures of child angels should be kept in the eastern corner of the house. A sacred heart picture of Christ should be maintained in the same corner for getting rid of negative forces in this home.

Vedic Building Code #4

This is an extremely large home. Usually these buildings are divided into several units. Sometimes part of it is rented. It is a home that requires constant maintenance and work. People living in these homes are always trying to build their lives upward, and the women of the home are constantly complaining that their domestic work is never finished. There is always a presence of religious statues and pictures in this home. The individuals living in this home work very hard for very low income. However, their life takes an upward trend very slowly and surely. A picture of Buddha or Christ in a meditative posture should be maintained to avoid quarrels in the home between couples.

Vedic Building Code #5

Sex, romance and love are very prevalent in this home. The negative qualities to look out for here are deceit, fraud, and false hopes. Women in this come are usually very attractive in appearance. People in this home also who are spiritual are constantly traveling. Almost everyone in this home owns a car and in some cases one person may own two cars. The couple who lives here are also very loving and the women are extremely beautiful looking. The men in this home are usually not fat. This home can also be a very lucky one for conducting business or professional services. There are also very high negative forces that can affect the individual in this home if they are not spiritual. Usually these homes have many cars or are surrounded by cars. People living in this home should avoid having illicit affairs or lustful thinking. A picture of Solomon or the angel Gabriel should be maintained in the eastern corner.

Vedic Building Code #6

Disagreements, quarrels, tension and responsibilities are the effects felt in this home. People living here who are lazy or irresponsible will suffer extremely hard emotional feelings in this home. Negative people will end up quarrelling with each other. Husband and wife will sleep separately from each other. Financial problems could become a reality if red meat is maintained as a regular part of the diet. Health can also be affected and if the payments for mortgage are not maintained, the residents of this home could end up in foreclosure. To avoid all these negatives constant meditation should be maintained. A special room should be dedicated to the Lord, as this house is an extremely large one. Tempers should be controlled. Duty should be the priority of all the residents in this home and a picture of John the Baptist should be maintained in a Christian home.

Vedic Building Code #7

This is a very large home also. A religious person or persons live in this home. The residents here are very slow in their actions and very laid back in their lifestyle. If a negatively rich individual owns this home, drugs, alcohol, and other addictions become prevalent here. Many of the activities in this home can be very secretive and the residents are constantly thinking or worrying about something. A positive effect on the house is that the residents here sleep very well and usually the beds are very large. Religious persons living here are usually very peaceful and are protected by divine forces. People in these homes should avoid criticizing and gossiping about others. Also, a picture of the cross without Christ should be maintained in the eastern corner of the home. A picture of Christ on the cross should be maintained in north side of this home.

Vedic Building Code #8

This is an extravagant, luxurious and large home. This can be an apartment building, a duplex or a home with several floors. The individuals in this home are extremely rich. Their income is high. Their furniture is expensive and their bills are high. Money comes very easily to the residents of this home and if negative, expenses will come instead. If the residents of this home are negative or have been cruel to others, eventually they are struck with serious sickness or diseases as a result of karma.

For good luck the individuals should avoid excessive gambling or drinking or waste. For religious individuals, a picture of the brilliant Sun should be maintained in the eastern corner of the house. A picture of full moon should be maintained in the same position. People in the house are involved in some kind of business or investment.

Vedic Building Code #9

This is usually a very large home, which is very expensive and which requires a lot of maintenance. If a negative person lives in this house, he or she will most likely suffer from an incurable disease. It is important that anyone living in this house should follow all religious rules of living and they should at all cost avoid eating red meat, drinking alcohol or taking drugs. It is also very important that an altar of God be maintained in this home so as to avoid all problems. People in these homes tend to become famous or well known in their community. Childbirth could be difficult during the months of pregnancy. Most of the individuals living in this home seek knowledge and other interests related to religion, astrology and philosophy. It is important that a picture or statue of all the angels and deities be maintained in this home in the eastern corner and Christians should have a shrine dedicated to the saints of the Old Testaments.

An Ideal Home for an Ideal Couple

Who is a gentleman? Any educated person may be a gentleman. But without having a legitimate wife, even an educated man cannot be gentleman. And after marriage, life cannot run without money. But no one gets money without efforts. Hence, marriage and taking up some economic occupation are necessary to be a civilized man. A civilized man must also make his residence at an excellent inhabitation, which is managed well. There must be water near the dwelling and the general environment must be as clean and pure as possible.

There must be two portions in a gentleman's house – one for storing necessary provisions and the other for sleeping. His bedroom must have a comfortable bedstead with soft cushions and white sheets. All the cosmetics must be handy in the bedroom. Apart from musical instruments, music system posters of natural scenes and love scenes of couples must decorate the bedroom.

The house must also have a swing, a lawn and a kitchen garden. The woman must use the inner portion of the house. It should have a bedstead with soft cushion. There must also be a smaller but comfortable bed nearby for lovemaking.

The owner of the house must enjoy physical intimacy with his wife on this smaller bed. Light snacks and drinks must also be handy in this room.

After a hard day's work, the evening of a gentleman must start with music. Guests may visit him at his time or the gentleman may visit someone else as a guest.

Chapter 14

THE VEDIC HOME CODE

How Your Home Affects Your Life

The house or apartment will affect each person differently according to his or her Vedic birth code. Add the Vedic Building Code to your Vedic Birth Code and you will obtain the Vedic Home Code. For example, if your Vedic Birth Code from Chapter 6 is #5 and your Vedic Building Code above is #6 then the Vedic Home Code is #2, i.e. (6+5=11 which is 1+1=2).

Now we will provide a description on how your life will be affected by the location or the place where you live. This will be revealed by the Vedic Home Code. The following table will help you quickly to obtain your Vedic Home Code.

TABLE 14:1- VEDIC HOME CODES									
BUILDING	YOUR VEDIC BIRTH CODE								
CODE:	1	2	3	4	5	6	7	8	9
BldgCd#1	2	3	4	5	6	7	8	9	1
BldgCd#2	3	4	5	6	7	8	9	1	2
BldgCd#3	4	5	6	7	8	9	1	2	3
BldgCd#4	5	6	7	8	9	1	2	3	4
BldgCd#5	6	7	8	9	1	2	3	4	5
BldgCd#6	7	8	9	1	2	3	4	5	6
BldgCd#7	8	9	1	2	3	4	5	6	7
BldgCd#8	9	1	2	3	4	5	6	7	8
BldgCd#9	1	2	3	4	5	6	7	8	9

Match your Vedic Birth Code on the top row to your Building or House Code in the left column then cross them to find your Vedic Home Code #. For example if your Vedic Birth Code is #2 and your House Location Code is #5, the Vedic Home Code is #7. Now check below for the forecast about how the house affects you under Vedic Home Code #7.

Vedic Home Code #1 - Life in This Home

You will feel independent, lonely sometimes and be bossy at home.

You will achieve high status in career and position in life.

You should be very spiritual in your thinking or you worry a lot.

You love to advise others; people will listen to your advice.

You will have a lonely child or you will feel pressured.

You always feel that others leave you alone a great deal.

Marriage partners are cautioned not to be too dominant.

You may become too independent for your partner's feelings.

You may worry a great deal; this may result in mental nervousness.

Vedic Home Code #2 – Life in This Home

You like to shop a great deal and look for bargains.

You cook tasty foods and food will always be in this house.

You may have a job that involves cooking while living here.

Make sure you serve all those who come here to reap good karma.

Anyone who visits you and is fed will bless you with prosperity.

You hate when your peace and quiet is disturbed in this house.

People see you as kindhearted and too helpful to others.
Others in the home will take advantage of your
kindness.
You will be involved in religious activities while living
here.
You will be involved in singing or may become a
famous singer.
Your partner in marriage makes a lot of demands for
attention.
You hate when anyone shouts at you here; it makes
you angry.
You will receive a lot of romance; too much for you
sometimes.

Vedic Home Code #3 – Life in This Home
Here you are usually skinny, small in stature and have
a thin waist.
You are argumentative and usually think you are
always right.
You may experience loss of children or have abortions
in your life.
Women here experience problems with regard to their
uterus.
They may also experience cramps, lower back pain or
bleeding.
You are childish in your ways; people think you are
immature.
You hesitate to accept responsibility but are forced to
do it.
You interact with the children a great deal.
You may be involved in publishing, writing or selling
books.
Your career may involve some form of telephone
communication.
You have many telephone lines or sets in this home.
There will be many computers or television sets in the
home.

You will be involved with videos, television and music publishing.

You may lose weight while living here; you will look 10 years younger.

You may have dental or plastic surgery done while living here.

You will feel very comfortable and lazy while living here.

Vedic Home Code #4 – Life in This Home

You will be very hardworking and conscientious while living here.

You may have a high temper because of many stressful moments.

You will be determined in your attitude and will not admit defeat easily.

If you want something done, you'll pressure others to do it immediately.

Too much work and overtime will affect your health.

It may take you a long time to buy a home, as you save money slowly.

Your income and expenses will most of the time be equal. Try hard to save.

You are always busy doing something in this home; rest a little.

Your mortgage may be high and your bills may be too stressful.

Back pain and stomach problems will affect you from working.

See the doctor regularly make sure your follow a spiritual life.

Vedic Home Code #5 – Life in This Home

You will change your mind a great deal and quickly in this home.

You love to travel and will travel to many places in the world.

Because your thinking is fickle it's hard for others to know your thinking.

You have intuitive powers and usually know things ahead of time.

You will be able to tell if others are telling false things to you.

You may be able know what others think about you by watching them.

You will be helpful to others by self-sacrifice, forgiving enemies easily.

You will help others without asking for compensation or money.

You will have a psychic and profound connection with the Universe.

You will counsel and advise friends and family in their business.

You are not very lucky with relatives; family members have no appreciation.

You will make friends easily; friends will help you the most in life.

The more good actions in life, the more beneficial it will be for you.

Being a vegetarian while living here will give you no health problems.

You may experience problems with the government, IRS or immigration.

While living here you will encounter many great spiritual personalities.

You will own more than one vehicle while living here.

Your job may involve traveling or driving long distances or using public transportation.

You will receive many long distance telephone calls or contacts from overseas.

Vedic Home Code #6 - Life in This Home

In this home you like to be in charge; you have a very strong ego.

Your job will thrust many responsibilities upon you.

If you fail to handle responsibilities while here, you will experience misery.

You may experience a lower or upper back pain, headaches or migraines.

Eating red meat in this home may lead to high blood pressure problems.

If not working for the government, you may have government problems.

Credit card problems, high mortgages and loans affect you here.

Make sure you pay all bills by cash while living here; avoid credit.

You may be able to have a business while living here; avoid loans.

You refuse to accept astrology, the occult or God very easily. Pray.

You feel very frustrated when you cannot have things your way.

You will experience inner fears and may think there is no help from God.

Avoid the color red or black as it brings surgery and health problems.

You may experience police or court problems while living in this house.

You could have many traffic tickets also while living here.

Your marriage will experience family problems while living here.

There will be fears of divorce or separation while living in this house.

You could experience robbery or burglary while living here.

Vedic Home Code #7 - Life in This Home

Your mind is running a thousand miles an hour while living here.

Your mind constantly thinks and analyzes everything.

You keep most of your thoughts to yourself; you hardly ever talk.

You will not tell your plans to other members of the household.

You feel you are right most of the time; you have a strong ego.

You will experience jealousy; you may think everyone is against you.

You appear very beautiful or handsome in the case of males.

You appear very sexy and attract the opposite sex very easily.

You have strong urges for love, sex and romance; you are very passionate.

If your spouse is negative you will ignore him or her a great deal.

A sure key to happiness for you is meditation, chanting and music.

You will make a good radio announcer, singer or religious leader.

You may become too kind hearted and will feel deceived by your lovers.

You should avoid the colors black and red; wear light colors.

You will become critical of others and gossip while living here.

You may have a fear of spirits while living here in this home. Pray.

You will meet many religious priests, psychics and astrologers while here.

Vedic Home Code #8 – Life in This Home

You love money and constantly think or quarrel about it.

You will have a business of your own at some point in this home.

Money flows through your hands very easily; try to save some.

If you are spiritual and conservative, the money will stay with you.

You may purchase expensive items and will be attracted to luxury items.

You will suffer from constipation problems and shortage of money.

You may become involved in fashions, modeling or designing.

You may have a strong ego and will feel that you are above others.

Investments in the stock market may prove to be profitable.

You will have money and will have people working for you always.

You love jewelry and may own of lot of it. Silver and pearls are good.

Avoid wearing anything black; this will kill your prosperity in life.

You will be attracted to movies, yoga, stock market, etc.

Vedic Hope Code #9 – Life According to Indra

You may have a high temper or a suspicious mind while living here.

You will experience the death of older family members.

Be careful of accidents and traffic violations while living here.

Alcohol will be very damaging to your life; avoid it in this home.

You may think very deeply about life and may become religious.

If you are positive person you could become popular or famous.

You may become involved in politics or become a leader.

You will become confused and will sometimes have many doubts.

Working for the government will be very beneficial for you.

You will struggle to fulfill your desires while living in this home.

You will spend more than you earn and bring financial problems.

You will be very fickle and impulsive in your actions in these houses.

Negative husbands may abuse their wives physically and mentally.

You will have a loud voice and will shout at others sometimes here.

The key to your happiness – donate yourself to work for charity.

You may spend your money without keeping some for the bills.

I hope each person, who has read the above, will use this information to help them buy the proper home by code so that happiness for the family can be experienced.

There are many times when a person has moved into a Vedic Building Code #9 home and has fallen ill immediately or a relative dies after the move. If you form a Vedic Home Code of #6 or #9 with a building address, then it is advisable that you do not move in the home until you have consulted with a Vedic Code advisor.

Chapter 15

The Vedic Sexual Code

The Cause of Human Creation

Like every creature, humans have received certain rights and certain duties for a successful existence in the world. Objects of comforts have also been provided. For human beings there are four objects for his existence. These are religion, luxuries, carnal pleasures and salvation. Most people neither crave nor strive for all four. The first three – religion, luxuries and carnal pleasures – are more important for them. These three objects are the basis of the word called love and are the basis for reason of existence. Everybody strives to achieve any of these objects with all his or her might. The discipline of love is a very difficult one to achieve and very hard to understand without the proper knowledge provided by the Vedic Code of Science.

Despite having enthusiasm, determination, faith and capacity, often a human being fails to achieve his object for the want of a competent partner. Sexual pleasure or carnal pleasure is one of the main objects of existence of a human being. But without a well-laid discourse and discipline, no one can achieve the best satisfaction in this pleasure. Like other disciplines, the Vedic Code of Love also contains certain norms and disciplined actions necessary to achieve one's goal.

Like religion and earnings, sexual satisfaction or carnal pleasure is the third goal of human life. Without having a proper knowledge of the Sexual Code, one cannot experience all the other physical comforts. A married person is naturally inclined towards carnal pleasures. In other words, carnal pleasures constitute the basic reason for marriage.

A man and a woman agree to tie a nuptial knot not only to have carnal pleasures but also to reproduce and provide continuity to the Universe. Marriage simply reflects the social nod for their union. The legal contract for the marriage only is an illusion. The real marriage takes place when the couples have been consummated sexually. The first date they make love with each other is considered the first day of marriage. Each time a woman makes love to a new man he is considered to be her husband in God's eyes. There are no city halls in heaven. A person entering a sexual union without knowing the basic knowledge about it, they will not be able to achieve the basic goal of marriage. It is here where The Vedic Code of Science comes in the picture. Evidences show that a sexual union of male and female forces had never been taken for granted even in ancient time. Ancient literature describe profusely about the authenticity, necessity and relevance of the Vedic Science of Sexual Codes and the necessity for sexual disciplines

Necessity of Education in Vedic Love Codes

The intelligent man in the olden days could enter married life only when he had thorough knowledge of Vedic Love Codes. His married life as result would be free from problems and conflicts.

Physical intimacy and sexual relations comprise the most delicate part of all human relations. In the words of well-known author, love seems to be the fastest thing, but it is the slowest thing to grow. Nonetheless, millions of people unite every year with the opposite sex. Some of these partnerships last a lifetime.

This section describes the kinds of the partners and agents who assist them in contracting with each other and establish physical relations.

Categories of Male and Female Partners

According to the size and depth of their private organs, male and female partners have been put in 9 categories according to the Vedic Birth Codes (from Chapter 6).

TABLE 15:1 - CHART OF BIRTH CODE vs. SEXUAL CATEGORIES			
VEDIC BIRTH CODES	MEN'S ANIMAL CODE	WOMEN'S ANIMAL CODE	HOW EACH VEDIC CODE PERSON REACTS TO SEXUAL ATTENTION AND LOVEMAKING
1	Tigers	Tigers	Agressive & Dominating & Selfish
2	Cow	Cow	Calm and Gentle , and Pleasing
3	Rabbit	Birds	Too much in a hurry, needs to slow down
4	Birds	Elephant	Slow and sure , sometimes very cold
5	Horse	Deer	Energetic, agressive and Pleasing
6	Lion	Elephant	Likes to play games, Ego can deny pleasure
7	Snake	Snake	Likes to experiment, full of stamina & desire
8	Deer	Rabbit	Loves fantasy and adoration..likes to act
9	Elephant	Tigers	Always ready for love but too suspicious

Rabbit, Snake and Bird males usually have a small phallus or in the case of females, small vaginas. Deer, Lion and Cow males have normal size phalluses and in the case of females, average vagina sizes, while Horse, Elephant and Tiger males have extremely large phalluses and in the case of females, deep or large vaginas. This information is very helpful when matching the marriages or sexual partners, as you can see if a Deer is matched to a Lion, it can be disastrous. Similarly if a Rabbit is matched to a Tiger it can be destructive.

TABOOS IN PHYSICAL RELATIONS

Of course, there is a strong attraction among the members of the opposite sex. This drive urges human beings to establish close physical contact with the opposite sex. But it won't be wise to have a physical relation with just anybody. There are certain taboos that give this behavior a direction, which a person should follow for saving themselves from sickness, death and suffering. According, one should avoid physical relations with the woman, who feels that she is better than all others or to a very low class woman, who is unclean and has bad habits. One should not long for a lustful relationship with a woman married to someone else. One should not have a relation with a woman who has been condemned by the societies, for it will damage your reputation.

Sound mental and physical health is the foremost necessity for establishing an intimate contact. A satisfactory physical relation between husband and wife is, in fact, the basis of a happily married life. Medicines are therefore required to remove physical ailments. Sages have developed certain Vedic of Science Remedies along with many herbal preparations to correct common physical ailments that lead to impotency in males and frigidity in females.

Lack of love and understanding between husband and wife is the most common mental problem that haunts most couples. Without love, no physical contact can bear fruits no matter how intimate it is. Hence, mutual love and understanding is also necessary to achieve peace in married life. Here, spiritual measures come in the picture.

Kinds of Lovers and Partners

For the purpose of procreation and continuity of the Universe, female partners are created with sexual attraction in mind. The woman's body is the objective desire of every man. Even wise sages and ancient gods fell prey to the beautiful and scantily clad women enchanted by lustful desires. There are mainly 9 kinds of male and female partners. These are determined by the Vedic Birth Codes.

TABLE 15:2 -CHART OF BIRTH CODE vs. SEXUAL CATEGORIES	
VEDIC BIRTH CODES	TYPES OF LOVERS AND PARNERS ACCORDING TO VEDIC BIRTH CODES
1	Dominating, Agressive, Insatiable, Leading and Hungry
2	Devoted, Willing lover, Always ready for love, Very giving
3	Playful, Tricky, Cunning, Hungry for love, Wants all attention
4	Cold, Passionate when aroused, Can be very passive, Dedicated
5	Fantasy-driven, Aggressive, Energetic, Creative and inventive
6	Egotistical, Selfish, Aggressive, Calculating and commanding
7	Secretive, Embracing, Kinky, and Demanding/Picky, Particular
8	Business-like, Wild, Dressy, Egotistical, Sometimes cold
9	Energetic, Aggressive, Demanding, Suspicious, Permiscuous

The Prostitute Lover falls in the 8th, or 6th or 9th category above. The Single and Widow Lovers can be the 1st or 7th or 9th category and the Dedicated Partners can be mostly 2nd, 3rd, 4th or 5th categories. Please note: I said Dedicated Partners not Lovers, as a woman or man may still be a dedicated partner, but if he or she does not get enough sexual attention at home then having a sexual lover outside the marriage is not completely ruled out.

Men must also take notice that if a woman is a widow, the Vedic Code of Science advises that her second or third husband or lover will die also, since there are planetary afflictions located in her uterus area for a long period of time. The spouse must also remember that the lovers in the 1, 6, 7, 8 and 9 categories are always in need of sexual attention and if not provided will look for other lovers.

Hence, in the next chapter, The Vedic Code of Science presents an ideal method of assessing your sexual compatibility using the Sexual Compatibility Code and a way to understand how you can please your partner with complete satisfaction by understanding their sexual needs and fantasies.

Chapter 16

Sexual Compatibility Code

Using the Vedic Code of Science we can add the Birth Codes of the two people and obtain the Vedic Love Code to determine how the couple will enjoy their lovemaking sessions. Again, from Chapter 6, take your Vedic Birth Code and add it to your partner's Vedic Birth Code. For example if your Birth Code is #5 and your partner's Birth Code is #2 then adding the two will result in a Vedic Love Code of #7 (5+2).

Sexual Compatibility Code #1
1-9: In conjugal relationship, the sensual aggressiveness of the #1 man matches the passion and submissiveness of the #9 woman. If the man is #9, he is impulsively passionate and the inventive and demonstrative. A #1 woman will match him perfectly.

2-8: When the man is #8 and the woman is #2 adjustment would be better if they reversed their roles. The tough and practical #8 man pursues a life of material satisfaction and the personality of the soft and cooperative #2 woman remains eclipsed. She does not quarrel and is happy with taking the backseat when he shows love and affection. She likes the protection and security provided by her partner.

3-7: Sexually, it is surprising to find #7 not reserved but a sensual and demonstrative person. The #3 is known to be warm and passionate and should enjoy the ecstasy of lovemaking very much. Inventions of #7 and impulses of #3 make them a well-matched team in the game of love.

4-6: Vedic #4 and #6 are fairly compatible in sexuality. Concerning their love life, both are generous, faithful, considerate and romantic rather than give away to animal passion. There is a satisfaction and happiness for both of them. Vedic #6 is more inclined toward lovemaking and #4 is fully supportive.

5-5: With regards to #5 and #5. The two #5's put together will be the worst possible combination and should be avoided as much as possible whether in personal life or in business. Each one of them has a love for freedom and cannot have parallel thoughts. Both of them are highly-strung, changeable and restless. If they live or work together, a disaster is imminent. Sexual attention becomes difficult even though both want it all the time, they cannot agree because of ego.

Sexual Compatibility Code #2
2-9: Both of them are imaginative, charitable, faithful, kind and affectionate. The inferiority complex of #2 is nicely covered and positive by the charm and forgiveness of #9. The #9 abides nicely with the suspicion, moodiness, sensitivity and creativity of #2. Impulsiveness and being prone to accidents are the negative points of #9, but the #2 learns to live with them. They enjoy conjugal bliss, share beautiful thoughts and enjoy each other's company. Passionate 9 longs for making love and #2 cooperates fully.

3-8: The two of them have personalities with serious differences and frequent chances of clashes. Both of them are ambitious but #3 is easygoing and not serious. On the other hand, no man in general and #3 in particular would be able to tolerate the authority of the #8 woman. On the intimate side, #8 is strong in lovemaking and #3 is warm, impulsive and adventurous. But #8 is jealous and moody and #3 can have extramarital relations if #8 is non-cooperative for very long.

4-7: A very good combination because of the balance in their natures. Both of them are calm, good-natured, non-argumentative and pleasant in their dispositions. Number 4 is practical, hardworking and trustworthy, providing security to the #7 woman, which she loves. On the intimate side they are found to be so well matched at all levels of expression – mental physical and spiritual – that perhaps they enjoy maximum ecstasy in lovemaking compared to any other couple.

5-6: One of them is hot tempered while the other one is of a cool temperament and consequently they seem to improve in time. The #5 may take risks, traveling, meeting people, given to pleasure of life, and try to convert the clever-minded impulsive #6 into accomplishing worthwhile goals. In their private life, #6 is loving and considerate but not sexually inclined. On the other hand #5 is more sexually inclined and insatiable, whether male or female. Either #6 has to fully cooperate with #5 having no personal demands or turn a blind eye towards its extramarital relations. It may be possible, if #5 is the male but perhaps difficult it is the female. This is the negative side of their relationship.

1-1: Both persons have the nature of leadership and self-concern. Each one may try to outdo the other in a never-ending game and it is anybody's guess who will be the winner. The solution can be found in compromise and cooperation by dividing the duties and privileges etc. This would be easier in a business partnership but not so easy in love and marriage where both have the prestige of their jobs on the one hand and dealing in household chores on the other. They may make an allowance for freedom to each other as far as seeking pleasure is concerned and won't be much worried about what that the other one is doing and where.

2-9: Both of them are imaginative, charitable, full of faith, kind and affectionate. Number 9 has the love of mankind and wants to serve and lift the humanity to a higher goal. Tolerance, compassion and forgiveness are its ornaments. Number 2 is romantic, quiet and cooperative although shy and lacking confidence initially. The two enjoy conjugal bliss, share beautiful thoughts and enjoy each other's company. Passionate #9 longs for making love and the #2 cooperates fully.

Sexual Compatibility Code #3

3-9: A very good combination of odd numbers leading to a successful union. Both of them have charm, which attracts each other. The #3 man at times can be obstinate and bossy but the #9 woman is tactful enough to handle him. Their conjugal bliss is perfect since both of them are romantic, warm and passionate and they like each other. They would never like to be separated from each other.

4-8: Both of them have similar viewpoints in life – practicality, hard work, intelligence, calmness and an urge to make a very good material and financial base for their lives. They make a successful team, achieving a lot in life, provided #8 does not push #4 too hard. Number 8 at times can be selfish, aggressive and might consider quarreling as normal. Number 4 is reliable, calm and charming. The bullying, cajoling and love of luxury and grand life style of the #8 may upset and disturb the #4 beyond repair, and this combination can result in failure. Number 8 is loyal and devoted but on the surface it finds difficulty in the expressing emotion or affection. At times it is moody and possessive and can hurt the feelings of the systematically affectionate and calm #4. Only occasionally can they make love to each other with satisfaction. This is a sore point in their relationship.

5-7: One thing, which both of them like, is to travel – a common factor, while in all other departments they must have a working compromise for successful living.

1-2: An ideal combination, especially if the man is #1 and the woman is #2, drawn to each other as opposites attract. The #1 man is dominating while #2 woman is submissive and they complement each other very well. The #2 woman is romantic, loyal, a born hostess, passive and always willing to do what a man wants. She will wait for him in the evening, look after him and give him conjugal bliss and assist him in all family dealings. She too is quite content because he gives her whatever she wants. She should not give chance for jealousy or provocation by her behavior otherwise there can be serious problems.

6-6: An ideal pair, completely in tune with each other, demonstrating love, beauty, happiness and a completely balanced family and home life. They do not need a probation period to decide on marriage. Their intuition tells them that they are made for each other. In lovemaking, they have better satisfaction in admiring, showering affection and caring for each other rather than getting involved in physical union every time. But nonetheless they enjoy perfect conjugal bliss.

Sexual Compatibility Code #4
2-2: Made for each other, identical in most of the ways, this combination is a symbol of perfect happiness. They would never like to away from each other even for short periods as they both like sex all the time at the least opportunity they have...if they do not have a quarrel. They enjoy a conjugal relationship. Both of them are romantic and compassionate, enjoying each other's company as they enjoy their sexuality.

5-8: A very strong combination – #5 is adventurous, resourceful, and impatient, while #8 is materialistic, practical and strong.

1-3: Number 1 and #3 are quite suitable to each other and they should make a good couple. The #1 man has leadership qualities whether at work or in the home. He would like his mate to be smart, well dressed and charming, which the #3 woman is. She is talented and versatile and is very well satisfied with the masculinity of the #1 man. If the man is #3 and the woman is 1 they make the same good couple with slightly interchanged roles. Both of them are lively and intelligent and can share very well the thoughts and feelings of each other.

4-9: On the personal side they make a slow but well developed relationship. Both of them are patient, understanding, compassionate and idealistic. In other respects they suit each other well. Number 4 can teach practically, hard work, and reasonableness in emotions and handling of money with care. Number 9 can teach spirituality, large mindedness, philanthropy and development of creative ideas. Number 9 is romantic, impulsive and demonstrative while #4 is systematic and orderly although loving and considerate but not adventurous. Hence if #9 learns to keep in check and is careful, the two of them will experience happiness and great joy in lovemaking.

7-6: The relationship is not a promising one if the man is 6 and the woman is #7. The #6 man is artistic and loving and looking for closeness and companionship. He would like to start the day with an affectionate kiss and would like to see his partner waiting for him for a warm fondling and a kiss when he returns home. When the man is #7 and the woman is #6 the situation is reversed with respect to their roles. The #7 man is imaginative, studious, philosophical, good-natured, dignified, and does not care for material or financial status very much. He finds a complementary union with the peaceful, quiet, loving and home loving #6 woman. Both of them are attracted to each other and they make a happy couple. Number 7 is the masculine number suited to a woman. They do surprisingly well with each other. Passionate and demonstrative, #7 man and romantic though spiritual #6 Woman enjoy their copulation.

Sexual Compatibility Code #5

1-4: This relationship is not recommended due to conflicting personalities and different views and opinions, and the compatibility is not likely to be there. There will be distrust and false accusations most of the time. They are generally indifferent in sex. Sex will be their downfall. The #1 woman likes a lot of excitement and adventure while the #4 man is the reverse.

2-3: The #2 man is kind, thoughtful and always willing to adjust and help. The two of them will start on a harmonious note and the going is good. But with the advancement of time, the #3 woman will find her beyond his limits, proud, independent, and definitely suspicious her of extramarital relations. And the #3 woman at no cost is going to bear the accusations. The relationship is not likely to last long. In case the man is #3 and the woman is #2, the combination is likely to be good and lasting, with their roles interchanged. The #3 man will easily have his way to find #2 woman to be good for him since she is timid, loving and perfect housewife. For her, he is a he-man giving her complete satisfaction. On the intimate side, one of them is romantic and tender (2) while the other is charming, versatile and warm (3) and the two complement each other very nicely. Although the physical side of the union may not be important for them, they will still have a regular sex life with each other.

4-9: On the personal side they make a slow but well developed relationship. The greatest fault of #9 is impulsiveness and irritation, although forgiving and never jealous. Number 4 is sensitive and can be melancholic at times. Number 9 is romantic, impulsive and demonstrative while #4 is systematic, orderly although loving and considerate but not adventurous. Hence if #9 learns to keep a check and is careful the two of them will experience happiness and great joy in lovemaking.

5-9: A partnership that can be very good at times and very bad on other occasions. Whenever it is the good, the credit goes to the visionary, spiritual and determined to live for others (#9). And whenever there are differences and problems it is due to the excited, high strung and self-indulgent #5. Number 5 should check its impulses and #9 its prejudices and moodiness. The sexy and adventurous #5 and emotional, passionate and visionary #9 should enjoy the ecstasy of copulation except when they feel out of sorts, because there might be disastrous nights.

6-8: The home loving #6 man and career-minded and materialistic #8 woman can strike a working balance if they accept each other's nature as such. The #8 woman is ambitious, strong and will do anything to achieve worldly things, money and power. The #6 man is quiet, loving, peaceful, artistic and creative. If both of them agree to his staying at home and her working anywhere in the world, including late hours at times, then the relationship can be successful. But the #6 man can be jealous and suspicious. Number 6 is the lover while #8 is moody and needs coaxing for lovemaking. Moreover, #8 is jealous and possessive but the smothering treatment of #6 brings the best out of it and they are likely to enjoy their copulation. The credit goes to the tolerant and affectionate #6, whether man or woman.

7-7: Both of them think, act and feel in the same way, completely in tune with each other, forming a stable and harmonious relationship. Both of them are brilliant, peace loving, non-argumentative, philosophical and studious. At times, they can be optimistic and confusing because of laziness or aloofness. On them intimate side, both of them are imaginative, demonstrative and passionate. There is neither suspicion nor jealousy, and they are in tune with each other. They enjoy lovemaking on the mental, physical and spiritual planes equally. There is happiness and bliss between them.

Sexual Compatibility Code #6

1-5: The two cannot go together for a long time. Number 1 is determined steady and career minded while #5 is versatile, changeable and sexy. The relationship is still worse when the man is 1 and the woman is #5. The #5 woman does not marry early in life unless she has had pre-marital relationships. It is only their private life, which may keep them together if they can compromise on other issues. The #1 man is strong, demonstrative and adventurous while the #5 woman can adjust in matters of sex. So the two can be suited to one another. If the man is #5 he is more prone to sex but the 1 woman too can adjust and the two can make a good couple.

3-3: Both of them are talented, versatile, and lively but restless and cannot settle down. They are proud, do not like to be obligated to others, are outspoken and love personal freedom so much that any joint venture appears a limitation and is likely to be unsuccessful. In private life, both of them being passionate and impulsive, enjoying conjugal bliss galore though neither of them is jealous or possessive of the other. Family members interfering in their private lives will constantly haunt them. They will long for some sex time and will hide to get some privacy.

2-4: A destructive and sometimes unbalanced relationship brings out the worst in each other. The #2 man is sometimes shy and diplomatic, and likes to avoid conflict at any cost. The #4 woman is practical, a born organizer, and is sometimes cold and cheap. She will, however, save for the future. When it comes to sexuality, the #4 woman can be very cold and unemotional towards her partner. The #2 man demands a lot of sexual attention, and the #4 woman refuses to provide that attention as much. This may result in the separation of beds or a divorce. Both individuals in this relationship may have been previously married. For this marriage to work, both partners need to put their egos in check and avoid involving family members in their affairs.

6-9: A well balanced relationship, both of them being artistic, talented, loving, tolerant, and understanding of each other's needs. It is a rare combination of beauty, domesticity, trust and devotion on the one hand of #6 and high mental and spiritual power, truth, philanthropy and love of mankind on the other #9. They should make a wonderful team because they understand each other at all levels of consciousness. They find enjoyment at both levels of consciousness-spiritual and physical. Both of them are romantic, patient, and considerate but with greater emphasis on the mental union rather than the physical. Nevertheless, #9 is passionate and impulsive while #6 is warm and affectionate, and there should be a tint of happiness and fulfillment in their copulation.

7-8: Number 8 is strong, ambitious, career-minded, and will not settle for anything until power and position is attained. Number 8 is resourceful, self-disciplined, ruthless and aggressive and can be selfish under negative circumstances. Number 7, on the other hand, is intuitive, studious, non-materialistic, meditative, and more often than not would try to adjust with the hot temperament of

#8. Number 7 can be aloof and secretive, raising suspicion and jealousy about involvement and whereabouts in the mind of #8. By nature, #8 is moody, living in extremes by luck. In copulating there can be serious ruffles if #8 is jealous and suspicious. But the emotional and passionate #7 can coax and bring about a harmonious sexual relationship if the #8 is in an extremely cold mood.

Sexual Compatibility Code #7
3-4: There are personality clashes between the two and a lot of allowances and compromises are necessary if the relationship is going to stay. It will depend on how much they can care for each other. In arguments, #3 normally wins. The impulsiveness and variety of #3 can never get along with the stability and the consistency of #4. On the physical plane they seem to make a good team and this is a strong point in favor of their stability in relationship. Number 3 is passionate, impulsive and demonstrative while #4 is sensitive and sentimental to the needs of love. They enjoy their copulation and this makes up for any differences in other spheres of life.

1-6: A balanced and well-adjusted couple that complements the needs of each other. The #1 man is demonstrative and adventurous while the #6 woman is romantic and chivalrous, and the two adjust well to each other's needs. If the man is #6, he is romantic and demanding while the affectionate and demonstrative 1 woman adjusts.

2-5: The relationship is sexy and adventurous. The #2 is a dedicated housewife and the #5 is an adventurous lover and faithful husband. He will sometimes have to be away from her but will miss her a great deal, and so will she him. When they do get together they will make passionate love together and will enjoy a loving companionship. The #2 must be careful, as her stinging words can be like arrows that will split the heart of her lover. This can make him disheartened, causing sexual inadequacy and loss of sexual satisfaction.

7-9: The two intuitive numbers – imaginative and mysterious #7 combined with the humanitarian and spiritual #9 – represent a supernatural union expressing peace, harmony and happiness for the couple. Both of them are non-materialistic visionaries, mostly away from the physical world, getting too abstract at times. In copulation both of them are imaginative, romantic and demonstrative. Number 9 is passionate and impulsive while #7 is emotional and demanding. They derive the maximum happiness.

8-8: Both of them are equally strong, dynamic, restless and ambitious. They can work tirelessly to achieve power, position and money. They are least concerned with love, harmony or setting a peaceful home. Whenever they work together for a common goal, they reach great heights in accomplishment, which can be a standard example in the world of materialism. And whenever either of them differs from the line of interest there can be chaos and total disaster. In private life both of them are suspicious, jealous and hard in the expression of their affections. They have changing moods and may be seen gentle and romantic one moment and cold and unconcerned the next. Each of them may be spying on one another. They need to reassure each other of their fidelity. However there are rare occasions when both of them are in the right moods for their lovemaking.

Sexual Compatibility Code #8
1-7: The two of them live a harmonious life. Number 1 is a doer, career minded, independent and purposeful, fitting very well with #7, who is intelligent, mysterious and intuitive, supporting each other for further development.

On the intimate side the #1 man is passionate and demonstrative and knows how to adjust with the #7 woman. She is neither jealous nor possessive and can use her imagination and intuition to suit her partner. On the other hand if the man is #7 he makes use of his romantic emotionality to combine with the demonstrative nature of the 1 woman. Both of them derive satisfaction on the physical as well as spiritual plane.

2-6: Both of them are evenly balanced, peace loving, passive, romantic and home-loving people, making a very promising couple. Both of them like beauty, harmony and entertaining guests. Number 6 is the caretaker and a natural host/hostess while #2 is the peacemaker. Their home should be well-decorated and full of beautiful things. In private life both of them are gentle, romantic and sentimental, caring more for emotional satisfaction and peace of mind than physical union or the animal passion. The #6 is an evergreen lover – no matter the age – and #2 is romantic. They can spend hours saying nice things to each other. They treat lovemaking very casually and not as a necessity.

3-5: A lot of action and entertainment for the watchers can be found between these two individuals, who are full with energy and restlessness. The #3 man is talented, charming, optimistic, lucky, and likes very much to enjoy the pleasures of life. The #5 woman is very well suited to him since she loves adventure and variety herself. But her love of freedom and taking risks makes her do whatever pleases her and the #3 man cannot contain her. Hence the brakes have to be applied to their speeds, if they want their relationship to remain good. When the man is #5 and the woman is #3 they are more suited to each other. He is adventurous, restless, and needs stimulation every now and then. She is charming and joyous and is the best person to keep him stimulated constantly. Moreover, #5 is changeable and #3 is very lucky so the couple can make the best of every situation. Artistic and creative endeavors of the #3 woman can get a good boost through the constructive criticism of the #5 man. The two of them complement each other nicely, can make good money, and go a long way happily together. In private life there is a lot of excitement. Five is the number of sex, adventure and excitement. Three is the number of excitement, sensuality and pleasure. The two of them indulge in intense lovemaking. But whenever there is a sign of tiredness it shows more of the face of #3 and this can result in #5 wanting to seek pleasure somewhere else.

4-4: A very successful union because both of them are exactly the same – hard working, systematic, brilliant though slow, trustworthy, home loving and very careful in handling money. The negative points can be their non-materialistic interests and melancholic depressions at times. The first thing is taken care of since they are slow but sure and necessary finances grow automatically. The second thing is not for long periods, and gloomy moods are not so serious. From the physical aspect they do not care much for sensual pleasures and are very happy being faithful and considerate to each other. Mutual exchange of love is their policy. They may enjoy lovemaking at times but is not a prerequisite. Neither of them is jealous, suspicious or possessive.

8-9: Both of them are resourceful, charming and good organizers but #8 has the strong desire for power, position and money for self while #9 has the intense desire to serve and help others and work for a common cause. It is here that they differ from each other completely and their views conflict. The intimate side is a difficult one for these two. Number 8 is cold, jealous, suspicious and extremely emotional. Number 9 is charming, passionate and impulsive. If lovemaking is denied to #9 on a few occasions then he/she can be intolerant and furious. Number 9 can adjust with #8 in many things but in matters of sex #8 must be normal and not demanding.

Sexual Compatibility Code #9

1-8: This is a love/hate relationship between two giants, both of whom are strong, tough and fixed in character. They will always try to outdo each other unless they have control over their forceful natures. Both of them are far too proud to say sorry to each other. If #1 decides to use the charm and forgiveness and #8 decides to curb jealousy and mold the emotions cooperatively, the relationship can be a rounding success. Otherwise, it is likely to end in an unmitigated disaster – a divorce or separation is imminent. The #1 man is a passionate lover and if the #8 woman is equally inclined, their enjoyment can be mutual. But if the #8 woman is unprepared, the #1 man cannot force her. On the other hand, if the man is #8 and the woman is #1 she will have to find the right time for copulation. The #8 person should remember that the #1 person can find another partner if love is denied.

2-7: Both of them are imaginative, sensitive, creative, philosophical and spiritual, and likely to make a very peaceful and harmonious life together. Both of them hate arguments and might be equally interested in religious pursuits. The #2 is inclined to follow #7 in most ways, including the interests of #7. Differences can arise when the #2 expresses suspicion and jealousy in the form of accusing #7. The reservation on the one hand and relations with higher ups and people of positions on the other, which #7 has, may create doubts in the mind of #2 and may overreact at times. In such a situation, even a breakup is possible, but the charm and passion of #7 is likely to bring the situation under control. In the department of love, they are likely to have great joys and pleasures. The #7 will take the lead in lovemaking, especially if it is the man, and the #2 will eagerly and willingly respond to the advances of #7.

3-6: The two of them have a very similar nature, complementing each other, and they will pass any test of a good relationship. Both of them have love, charm, creativity and intelligence. There are some problems when the #3 is aggressive or financially wasteful. His #6 wife is cool and well balanced in economic matters and he will have to adjust a bit. Similarly, the #6 woman has to check her habit of taking on too many responsibilities of friends or relatives. The #6 man cannot think of another woman. The two of them make a very good couple.

4-5: 4 is practical and systematic while #5 is imaginative and freedom loving but adjustable. Although the two numbers do not have a common denominator but they are found to complement each other and make a reasonable pair with some adjustments. In private life the #5 person is known to be sexy and demonstrative while the #4 person is loving and considerate but not excited, so the #5 man should try to be gentle with the #4 woman. If the man is #4, he will have to be tactfully controlling the #5 woman and cooperate with her otherwise she finds a way out for her hot-blooded passions.

6-3: In the conjugal relationship the #3 person is passionate, demonstrative and adventurous while the #6 person is also capable of deep love but does not really respond. The #3 man may have to have some extramarital relations at the time, which the 6 woman will ignore since they continue to have a beautiful relationship based on love. If the man is #6, he is able to meet the needs of the #3 woman with his strong physique and romanticism. In general, this Vedic Sexual Code presents many hurdles in the couple's sexual life, but with a great deal of understanding and spirituality the couple can experience all the joys of sex in their life.

9-9: This is the relationship of the highest order, full of love, understanding harmony and with a burning desire for the common cause of humanity. Both of them are hard working, intuitive, intelligent, perfectly matched and balanced and knowing each other perhaps for more than a lifetime. They are in complete agreement with each other at all levels of consciousness – physical, mental, emotional, and in intuition. On the intimate side they are the fittest example of relationships. Both of them are loving, passionate and impulsive. The lovemaking brings both spiritual and physical satisfaction full of bliss and fulfillment.

So, there you have it – the explanation of the Vedic Sexual Codes. Hopefully you will have a better understanding of your partner's sexual needs and be able to satisfy him or her in a better way.

My forthcoming book, *Life Code 3: The Vedic Sexual Code*, will follow soon. This book explains the Vedic Sexual Code in greater detail and will be provide invaluable advice on making your sex and marriage life more enjoyable and fulfilling.

Chapter 17

The Marriage Code

Marriage is the foundation of the Universe. If there is no love, there is no marriage. If there is no marriage, there are no children and if they are no children, there is no world. If there is no world then, there is no God. Marriage keeps the world in a continuous cycle of birth and rebirth. Because marriage has such a great influence on our very existence, the sages and masters of the Vedic Code of Science declared that no marriage should take place without the advice of a wise master.

Every time two people get married, it is the merging of two families, two generations and the future of the world is at stake. A couple can bring forth a Christ that will save the world or a Hitler that can destroy the world. Each time a couple ties the knot, we will be affected by the outcome of that marriage. That is why we have so many ancient books advise us about marriage compatibility and so on.

Just like we have the seasons of winter, spring or summer, so also the timing of a union of two people determines the unhappiness or happiness of that marriage. Imagine for a moment if you were to plant a seed in the middle of winter, it would never germinate. You must plant it in the spring to assure growth. So also if a couple consummates a marriage at the wrong time, obstacles and destruction will present themselves.

Before we go into the discussion about the timing of marriage, we will first look at the matching of couples through their Vedic Birth Codes. It is important that couples know ahead of time how their marriage will be affected after their wedding and how to take steps to correct any negativity in advance so that they can live a happily married life. I hope this knowledge will assist in the elimination of the forces, spouses cheating on each other and the lack of love in people's lives.

To obtain your Vedic Marriage Code, you need to add your own Vedic Birth Code to that of your intended spouse. The Vedic Birth Code can be obtained in Chapter 6. For example, if your Vedic Birth Code is #2 and your intended spouse's Vedic Birth Code is #6, then the Vedic Marriage Code is the addition of the two (2+6) or Marriage Code #8.

TABLE 17:1 - VEDIC MARRIAGE CODE NUMBER									
PARTNER'S BIRTH CODE	YOUR VEDIC BIRTH CODE								
	1	2	3	4	5	6	7	8	9
#1	2	3	4	5	6	7	8	9	1
#2	3	4	5	6	7	8	9	1	2
#3	4	5	6	7	8	9	1	2	3
#4	5	6	7	8	9	1	2	3	4
#5	6	7	8	9	1	2	3	4	5
#6	7	8	9	1	2	3	4	5	6
#7	8	9	1	2	3	4	5	6	7
#8	9	1	2	3	4	5	6	7	8
#9	1	2	3	4	5	6	7	8	9

Match your Vedic Birth code on the top row to the spouse's Vedic Birth Code on the left column and cross them to find your Vedic Marriage Code. Then check below for the forecast about the marriage under all of the Vedic Marriage Codes.

Vedic Marriage Code #1
A fairly neutral marriage.
A marriage that will create loneliness and independence
    for both.

One partner will feel lonely and rejected by the other partner.
Each partner worries about the other's welfare

Vedic Marriage Code #2

A very positive and excellent marriage.
Romance and true love
Cooperation
Each partner has a previous lover that they cannot
forget about
Can be destroyed by too much kindness to outsiders or
interfering family members

Vedic Marriage Code #3

A fairly positive and good marriage.
Communication problems
Ego problems; each partner thinks he or she is right
The couple will have problems with children and will
benefit or lose through them.

Vedic Marriage Code #4

A fairly positive marriage.
A very hard working couple
Will always have problems with tenants/landlords,
bank, and properties
The couple have many enemies and be the envy of
family and relatives
Will become wealthy but may lose it all because of ego
and pride.

Vedic Marriage Code #5

A very positive and good marriage.
But can be destroyed by illicit affairs and gossip
The couple does not mean what they say to the other
and usually makes sudden plans without letting the
other know.
Couple is concerned with bodily needs
Couple likes to impress their friends or family.

Vedic Marriage Code #6

A very negative marriage. It needs a lot of understanding.
Disagreements and court cases
Family interference and criticism of the couple by
  relatives
Constant battle over the children for custody

Vedic Marriage Code #7

A fairly calm and positive marriage.
Each partner thinks he or she is perfect.
A good partnership for spirituality, occult studies and
  religion
Ego problems causing intelligent arguments and
  disagreements
Helpers for temple and builders or religious organizations
Charitable and kind couple to all outsiders

Vedic Marriage Code #8

A very positive and excellent marriage.
Money will become the main issue of the marriage.
If the couple owns a business, they will live happy and
  prosperous.
Lust and greed for wealth can destroy the marriage.
The couples will experience ownership of real estate,
  big bank accounts and investments.
Both partners like to dress up with expensive clothes
  and jewelry.
The marriage will experience jealousy from females.
One of the partners will experience constipation
  problems.
One or both partners can experience fame or
  popularity.

Vedic Marriage Code #9

A very negative and destructive marriage.
A death of a relative or friend will occur as soon as the
  couple gets married or has sexual relations.

One of the partners will have a serious illness or
   disease.
Involvement in spiritual practices, temples, ashrams,
   and churches
Children and financial problems

Chapter 18

The Love Compatibility Code

This chapter is a short one that will help you determine if the person you met recently will be someone worth working towards marriage. In order to find this out, you need to know the birthdate of the person you are dating or the one you intend to marry.

On the following table you will find the Vedic Birth Code of the other partner in the top row. Match it to your Vedic Birth Code in the left column and then cross it to find the Vedic Love Code. After the table below, you will find the factors affecting these love connections.

TABLE 18:1- VEDIC LOVE CODES									
PARTNER'S BIRTH CODE	YOUR VEDIC BIRTH CODE								
	1	2	3	4	5	6	7	8	9
#1	2	3	4	5	6	7	8	9	1
#2	3	4	5	6	7	8	9	1	2
#3	4	5	6	7	8	9	1	2	3
#4	5	6	7	8	9	1	2	3	4
#5	6	7	8	9	1	2	3	4	5
#6	7	8	9	1	2	3	4	5	6
#7	8	9	1	2	3	4	5	6	7
#8	9	1	2	3	4	5	6	7	8
#9	1	2	3	4	5	6	7	8	9

Vedic Love Connection Code #1
Not a good love connection; it is considered fair but negative.
This connection could fail as a result of loneliness by
each partner.
Each lover makes the other one feel rejected.

Seek advice before getting married.

If this love connection leads to marriage it's because one partner does not want to let go of the other, which may result in separation mentally and also through illicit affairs.

Worrying and loneliness will have to be the acceptance for both partners before they can be happy.

Warning – If one partner is abusive in this connection, then marriage should be avoided.

Vedic Love Connection Code #2

An excellent combination for love connection.

What and how they speak to each other is important in the love connection.

Romance, music and food will determine the success of the love connection.

Love connection will last a long time and it will definitely lead to a happy marriage life.

Vedic Love Connection Code #3

An excellent combination for a love connection.

Childish and immature quarrels can lead to divorce or separation.

If the partners don't have a sense of humor it will lead to disaster.

Children and childish ego control by one partner can destroy this marriage.

Any abortion prior to the marriage will destroy the relationship.

This love connection will result in marriage and the wedding will be like a great party.

Vedic Love Connection Code #4

Not a good love connection; it is considered fair but negative.

This love combination needs a lot of effort to make it successful, as each partner will suffer a lot of stress from each other.

Career choices and hard work will be the factors for
    happiness.
This connection will lead to marriage.
Because of stress each partner should try to look after
    each other's health.

Vedic Love Connection Code #5
An excellent combination for a love connection.
Extramarital affairs or each partner not wanting to be
    wrong can destroy this love connection.
This connection may not lead to marriage as a result of
    distrust.
Each partner must learn to trust each other before
    marriage.
Sexual encounter will occur prior to marriage.
A decision for marriage may come up too early.
If each partner does not try to overtake each other's
    freedom the love connection will become fruitful.

Vedic Love Connection Code #6
This is a very negative love connection combination
    and must be carefully monitored.
Family is the greatest trouble and blockage if allowed
    to interfere in the couple's life.
This love connection may not lead to marriage as a
    result of family interference.

Vedic Love Connection Code #7
A good love connection that can be destroyed by ego.
Each partner is looking for a perfect spouse and there
    is no such thing as a perfect person.
This can lead to love connection but a lot of effort is
    needed for communication between the two.
This connection will lead to marriage and can become
    very happy if the partners are very spiritual.

Vedic Love Connection Code #8

An excellent combination for a love connection.

Money, luxury, and investments will affect this love connection.

The wedding ceremony will be of grand scale.

Extramarital affairs or each partner not wanting to be can destroy this love connection.

This connection will lead to marriage and can be very happy.

Vedic Love Connection Code #9

This is a very negative love connection combination and must be carefully monitored.

This love connection is not recommended unless proper precaution is taken.

Death of a family member, sickness, and financial problems are all factors that can follow this combination.

For the love connection to work properly each partner will have to be vegetarians, avoid alcohol and bath in ocean waters frequently.

This connection may not lead to marriage but if it does it may become a health-affected relationship.

Chapter 19

The Soul Mate Code

How to Know if Your Partner is Your Soul Mate From a Past Life

Déja vous! You have met this person somewhere in your past before...Are you sure?

Many times people experience the feeling that the person or place they are visiting generates memories that seem to indicate they were there before or knew the person before, even though they have never met in this life or visited this place. This feeling can represent some strange and weird emotions within one and can sometimes make a person feel uncomfortable, too. Because there is belief in reincarnation, this feeling is not uncommon among people but since some other cultures do not accept reincarnation, it presents surprises sometimes within the western person's mind. Many people have consulted with me as to why they are attracted to someone else with a strong passion even though they are married. This is because of something called "Karmic Connection" with that person in a previous life.

Generally everyone and everything we encounter in our life has a "Karmic Connection" with us, but we do not realize these effects unless the connection is very strong, such as in relationships with other people and special places. In this article, I present some of the ways of determining whether you and your partner are soul mates or whether a certain location is where you were before in your past life. If you and your partner have the same Vedic Birth Codes, then you are soul mates and were together in the past life.

Other factors that indicates previous life experiences can be determined by...

1 When both people have the same Vedic birthdays
2 When both people have the same Sun longitude of birth
3 When both people have the same Vedic Life Path Codes
4 When both people have the same Moon longitude degree of birth
5 When both people have the same first and middle name
6 When both people have the same birth star constellation degree of birth

Sometimes when sisters-in-law do not agree with each other and they become enemies, it is considered a "Previous Life Connection". When a mother-in-law gets a daughter-in-law that she dislikes, this may also be a Previous Life Connection.

There are repayment Karmic connections such as the right of a lamb that has been killed by a butcher in a previous life will be reborn in this life as a butcher, while the butcher has returned to this life as a lamb. Other connections like these are...

An employee who has been affected in a drastic way by a boss

A child that was only allowed to stay a month or less in the world so as to distress a parent who had aborted him before

A husband who was abusive to his wife in the last life to the point of making her an enemy in the last life, that he dies soon after love connection

A princess in the last life who is now married back to the
   prince but he ends up having many affairs because
   she had rejected him in the last birth.

And many more...

In the following paragraphs, a comparison of the same
Vedic Birth Codes of two people is determined and the
results thereof are given.

Vedic Birth Code #1 Married to Vedic Birth Code #1
Both persons have the nature of leadership and self-
concern. Each one may try to outdo the other in a never-
ending game, and it is anybody's guess who will be the
winner. The solution can be found in compromise and
cooperation by dividing the duties and privileges, etc.
This would be easier in a business partnership but not
so easy in love and love connection where both have the
prestige of their jobs on the one hand and dealing in
household chores on the other. The man cannot expect
the woman to be waiting for him to serve when he returns
home from work. They have to share everything on an
equal basis, unless the woman recognizes her femininity
and calculates a slight margin for adjustment.

Vedic Birth Code #2 Married to Vedic Birth Code #2
Made for each other, identical in most of the ways this
combination is a symbol of perfect happiness. The
#2 man is not extraordinary in any way but simple,
straightforward, secure, one who worries little with no
additional involvement, and who longs to come home
after work. And the #2 woman just waits for him to
return from work and look after him as the ideal man in
her life. She is not a career woman and may like to give
up her job after love connection to live as a housewife.
The two of them do not have to make up any excuse or
give any explanation for any shortcomings since they

understand each other. They would never like to away from each other even for short periods. Both of them have a touch of spirituality and their interests run almost parallel. At times there can be problems since both of them are shy, lack confidence, suspicious and jealous and quite often under depression.

Vedic Birth Code #3 Married to Vedic Birth Code #3
Soul mates, but highly negative. Strong family influence, families disagree on both sides of the love connection partners' family. Childish arguments by the partners usually involving insults to each other's family. Most of the fights will be about family. This love connection is subject to divorce.

Vedic Birth Code #4 Married to Vedic Birth Code #4
A very successful union because both of them are exactly the same – hard working, systematic, brilliant though slow, trustworthy, home loving and very careful in handling money. The #4 man will provide security to her, which she needs very much and the #4 woman will take care of him as a perfect housewife. Each of them is a builder and the two of them together will build an excellent home for themselves. The negative points can be their non-materialistic interests and melancholic depressions at times. The first thing is taken care of since they are slow but sure and necessary finances grow automatically. The second thing is not for long periods and gloomy moods are not so serious.

Vedic Birth Code #5 Married to Vedic Birth Code #5
Soul mates, but very difficult because of trust issues. Each partner tries to outsmart the other. Each personality thinks that the other won't know that they are doing. This relationship can be highly successful if each partner is honest with each other. The demand for sex is high on both sides. Communication is very important!

Vedic Birth Code #6 Married to Vedic Birth Code #6
These two are soul mates, but very childish in their ways. Constant arguments about silly things that are not important will dominate this relationship, if one or both partners are negative. They love children and their first child will always be a boy.

Vedic Birth Code #7 Married to Vedic Birth Code #7
Soul mates, they will always think of each other and can never forget their lovemaking moments. Highly egotistical relationship and can separate because of ego, but will constantly come back because of ego, because each partner wants to possess the other. Love connection is highly recommended for this combination.

Vedic Birth Code #8 Married to Vedic Birth Code #8
8-8: (*) Both of them are equally strong, dynamic, restless and ambitious. They can work tirelessly to achieve power, position and money. They are least concerned with love, harmony or setting a peaceful home. Whenever they work together for a common goal they touch great heights in accomplishment, which can be a standard example in the world of materialism. And whenever either of them differs from the line of interest there can be chaos and total disaster. For success either of them can be selfish and aggressive. When in tune both of them look charming and a dignified couple. Neither of them is unstoppable and unless real care is taken they can actually destroy each other.

Vedic Birth Code #9 Married to Vedic Birth Code #9
Soul mates, usually when these two people bring together negative things such as death and sickness happening in the family on both sides. It is highly recommended that a priest be consulted when a love connection between these two is about to take place. They both like to deny their own faults and thus this

can become a very negative relationship. Whenever a #9 personality comes into sexual contact with any other of the Vedic Birth Code, death will occur on one side of the family.

Chapter 20

The Fertility Code

The female uterus or womb acts as a separate organ of the body and is influenced highly by the movement of the Moon. The mouth of the uterus moves from side to side as the blood flow of the body is controlled by the gravitational pull of the Moon. Our blood consists of all the elements in the same proportion as the elements contained in the ocean. The movements of the Moon control the tides of the ocean as it travels around the world in approximately one month. So also the blood flow of the menstrual cycle of the female is affected on a monthly bases as the Moon controls the tides of our body's fluids.

Whenever a woman has menstrual cycle problems, cramps or back pain, it is an indication that the womb has been disturbed in its cycle of movements and is not in harmony with the Moon, gravitation, etc. This disharmony can present a lot of reasons for fertility problems, lovemaking difficulties, negative desire of a woman to be with her husband, anger between couples due to lack of sexual attention, etc.

The main reason the womb loses its harmony with the Moon's orbit is a diet that consists of red meat, because when we were children, we were fed the cow's milk, which caused our bodies to be built up with proteins from red meat. Eating red meat is like eating our own flesh. As this red meat enters your lower stomach, it will appear to be a part of your lower body to the Moon and so the Moon will think that it as part of your womb. This can cause a movement that is not in harmony with your uterus, thereby causing the mouth of the womb to move or twist in the wrong direction. This very movement can cause a bad sexual connection between husband and wife in lovemaking and therefore both couples will experience the feeling of dissatisfaction with each other. This will also prevent the sperm from reaching the egg.

In ancient times a wiser and older woman would massage the womb into positions using herbal oils so that the woman can become impregnated. Usually Western doctors notice a twisted womb, but would be unable to move it back into place. Only the massaging technique works. I have done these massages for many women who could not get pregnant by treatment from ordinary doctors. Now they are all pregnant and happy.

There are many other factors that create infertility problems. Usually if these factors are corrected then the fertility level of the couple will be increased.

The following Vedic Birth Codes (from Chapter 6) will indicate some possible measurement of the infertility level of the female or male involved. It will explain why some people are more fertile than others are. It also may help some of you understand why you are not able to get pregnant after trying so long. Finding out your Vedic Birth Code and reading the following under your Vedic Birth Code will help you apply to your life.

Vedic Birth Code #1
The fertility level is high and is considered positive.
The chance of becoming pregnant is 80%.
Most women of this category try to prevent pregnancy.
The mother will feel confined when the baby is born.
Because of the high fertility rate, young girls become
    pregnant easily.
Some mothers may abandon their children at birth.
Vedic Birth Code #2
The fertility level is high and is considered positive.
The chances of becoming pregnant are 100%.
Most women with is Birth Code usually do not like the
    labor pains and usually stop after 2 or 3 babies.
Women consider child rearing a job too hard for them,
    however they make the best mothers.

Vedic Birth Code #3

The fertility level is low and is considered negative.

The chances of becoming pregnant are 50%.

Women in this category experience many uterus problems so fertility is low sometimes.

They always experience a miscarriage or an abortion.

Chances are the mother of this person experienced an abortion and miscarriage also.

The more children they have the more prosperity.

The males in this category will experience premature ejaculation problems.

The women's wombs get twisted to the right easily thus causing infertility.

Abortion of the 1st child can create infertility problems.

Vedic Birth Code #4

The fertility level is average and is considered fair.

The chances of becoming pregnant are 70%.

The women in this category will find some peace with themselves after childbirth.

Usually they are very picky with their partners so children can come late in life.

Any childhood sexual abuse usually lowers the fertility level of the women.

These women form a deep spiritual bond with their children.

Vedic Birth Code #5

The fertility level is high and is considered positive.

The chances of becoming pregnant are 100%.

Most of these women experience some type of sexual abuse at a young age – if so, the fertility rate is lowered.

If not, then the fertility rate is high and a pretty baby girl is conceived quickly.

Abortion of the first child can prevent further conceptions.

Vedic Birth Code #6

The fertility level is low and is considered negative.

The chances of becoming pregnant are 60%.

Most women in this category will suffer from back pain; this will lower the fertility rate.

Back pain or migraines may come from a childhood accident or fall and can causes a twisting of the womb.

Red meat will also lower the fertility rate and cause miscarriages or inability to become pregnant.

Avoiding all types of meat can increase fertility level.

Massaging of the spinal cord can increase the chance of becoming pregnant.

The men in this case experience low sperm count or weak erections.

Vedic Birth Code #7

The fertility level is average and is considered positive.

The chances of becoming pregnant are 80%.

Women in this category have weak wombs, which act dormant or barren sometimes.

The reason for that is that there are more male hormones than female hormones in her body.

Usually the hairier the body, the lower the fertility level, and the less hairy the more fertile she is.

She must take hormonal treatment to increase estrogens.

Special herbs can be taken to increase chances of pregnancy.

Sitting in a tub of seawater can increase fertility level.

Sit-up exercises or massaging of the lower belly with oils can increase the chance of pregnancy.

Loss of head hair indicates low infertility.

Vedic Birth Code #8

The fertility level is low and is considered positive.

The chances of becoming pregnant are 65%.

The first being a girl most of the time the women experience many constipation problems.

Women in this category tend to use a lot of contraceptives and usually when ready to get pregnant, the fertility level is lowered.

Vedic Birth Code#9

The fertility level is average and is considered positive.

The chances of becoming pregnant are 70%.

The women of this category can get pregnant easily provided no childhood abuse occurred.

These are very energetic people who love to be with children always.

The women enjoy being pregnant sometimes and experience pleasure from breast feeding their babies.

The men in this category sometimes experience impotence or low sperm counts.

Please note that the female body contains its own fertility clock. After a woman has given birth to a baby, the impure blood continues to ooze out of her uterus for almost three months following the birth. She is usually infertile during that period of time. Also you must be aware that as long as the mother is breastfeeding the baby, the mother will not ovulate or menstruate until she stops breastfeeding the baby. As you can see, the female body has its own fertility control timer.

The Vedic Code of Science does not recognize menopause as a normal part of life. When a woman suffers from this complaint, it means that her womb has been affected by a sickness of some sort, and certain exercises and herbal treatments would be needed to fix the womb back into place so that the sexual sensitivity can be revitalized. In ancient times older women in the villages would treat women with this so-called "menopause" and wives would enjoy their husbands until they are way past the age of 60. So when the ovulation period stops, it does not mean the woman's love life is finished.

With regards to men, they will experience impotence or low sexual vitality if they do not eat a proper diet. Salt, onions, garlic, pepper and other stimulants will increase their energy for sexual attention. Herbs as well as all beans increase the chance of fertility.

Chapter 21

The Pregnancy Code

Is it a boy or a girl? If you are wondering about the gender of your first, second or third child after you get married or pregnant, this chapter will provide you with interesting insight as to how you can determine this through the Vedic Code of Science. Nowadays, with the common use of contraceptives, pregnancy-controlling mechanisms and abortion clinics, many people have changed their views about pregnancy. Imagine if the entire woman decided to get an abortion, then what would happen to the world? There will be no continuation of the Universe. Each time a person has an abortion in the world, it changes the whole makeup of the Universe. The aborted child could be an Einstein, a Newton or a Christ.

The first pregnancy of a couple forms the first flower that will bear fruit in that couple's life. Usually, if the child is aborted, the couple will break up or separate. General statistics show that most young couples, who aborted their first child, ended up separating from each other after that. Most disabled children born to married couples are usually preempted by an abortion. It is as if the aborted child came back again to punish the couple for have aborted it. The disabled child becomes the punishment or the task of the whole family from grandmother to mother and whomever else.

We all know that once the seed is planted and starts to grow, the path of karma taken by that growth cannot be changed, just like shooting an arrow cannot be stopped or change its course once it leaves the quiver.

In the following paragraph, using your Birth Code, observe the information about the type of child that you will have as your first, second or third, according to your Vedic Birth Code. Nature and the Universe has also provided some type of guidance as to how we can determine how our future children are going to be, depending on the amount of boys and girls in the woman's life. This information can be found after the first child is born in the afterbirth that follows. The afterbirth contains ribbed parts of pink and blue. The number of pink and blue parts of the afterbirth indicates how many boys and girls are scheduled to born in the woman's life. If a child is aborted, the count is included in the afterbirth.

Doctors are not aware of this method of knowing how many children a person should have, however, it is an ancient knowledge, which has been used in India for centuries. In this writing, we will provide some of that knowledge according to the Vedic Code of Science. You can find your Vedic Birth Code in Chapter 6 and use that code to find out about your children.

Vedic Pregnancy Code #1
The first child will be a boy depending on the love
    connection. If the husband has a Vedic Code of #7,
    the first child will be a girl.
If the first child is a boy, a girl will follow it.

Vedic Pregnancy Code #2
It is most definite that the first child will be a girl. The
    only chance to a boy can occur if the husband is a
    Vedic Code 3.
The second child will be a boy followed by a girl.
You usually have a problem after having the third child
    and may refuse to have more because of the labor
    pain or pressure of pregnancy.
Your children will protect you and take care of you
    later; you will benefit from them.

Vedic Pregnancy Code #3
Definitely it's a boy no matter what the Birth Code of
    the other partner is.

Second child will be a boy if the first child was
abortion or miscarriage.
People with this Birth Code always experience a birth
code or miscarriage.
If the first child is a boy and there is neither miscarriage
nor abortions, it will be followed by a girl.
The more children you have, the more prosperous your
life will be.
Usually there are more boys rather than girls.
Most of the people in this Birth Code may be denied
children as a result of family background karma.

Vedic Pregnancy Code #4

The first child is most likely a girl unless influenced by
the other partners.
The second child is most likely a girl followed by a boy.
Girls are lucky for you and so there will be more girls
than boys in your life.

Vedic Pregnancy Code #5

The first child is most likely a girl unless influenced by
the other partners.
You love your children and will treat them like adults.
Pregnancies are difficult and usually you may have
only one son and many daughters.

Vedic Pregnancy Code #6

The first child is most likely a boy if not influenced by
partner's Birth Code.
The second child is most likely a girl followed by a boy.
Most of the people in this Birth Code may be denied
children as a result of family background karma.
Special methods and operations may be needed for
pregnancy.
Most of the people under this Birth Code go through
Caesarian deliveries.

Vedic Pregnancy Code #7

The first child is most likely a boy if not influenced by
partner's Birth Code.

The second child is a boy and could be followed by a
girl.

Most of the children may be boys.

If the grandfather was abusive to women then all the
children will be just boys and no girls would be
allowed in the family.

Vedic Pregnancy Code #8

The first child is most likely a girl unless influenced by
the other partners.

Usually a boy may follow the first but most of the
children are girls under this Birth Code.

Usually these couples only prefer to have only two or
three children.

Vedic Pregnancy Code #9

The first child is most likely a boy if not influenced by
partner's Birth Code.

The second child is most likely a girl followed by a boy.

Most of the children may be boys.

There are possible abortions, miscarriages and
difficulties with pregnancy.

There are many factors that may affect the outcome
of a pregnancy. Vedic science teaches that the sex of the
baby can be changed by spiritual words called "mantras"
before the third month of pregnancy. In my work I have
been able to help many women have children, even
though the medical doctors had given up on them. I have
also noticed that if the first child is aborted, the child
following may become disabled for some reasons.

It is advisable that the first child should never be
aborted, as this pregnancy is the planting of the first
seed, so to speak, and is the first flower of love that

comes from the newly married lovers. The first baby will contain the essence of their love connections.

In my experience, I have also noticed a hereditary trait that affects the outcomes of pregnancy and that is that if a female child was abused, molested sexually or if she eats a great deal of red meat then the womb somehow becomes traumatized. Thus, she is unable to become pregnant after she gets married. In addition, if the father of any boy was a sexually illicit or perverse person, his sons will be denied female children.

My advice is always to make sure you check your family history thoroughly before assessing why you may be having problems with pregnancy.

Chapter 22

The Health Code

According to the Vedic Code of Science the healthiest human being is one who is blessed with inner peace, divine satisfaction with all that he/she has or possesses and the acceptance of all things in the Universe (living or non-living) as part of his/her living relationship. Health problems are indications that we are not living in harmony with our environment, that we are not living within the laws of nature and proper interaction with the Universe around us.

In my experience as a swami, I have noticed that our inner thoughts and the ways we express them to others as well as to the Universe create a returning reaction to us in the form of good or bad health problems. For example, I have found that people who have deceived others in their love life suffer from heart problems; a person who might have kicked others in anger may suffer foot problems; and a person who might have cursed others suffers mouth problems. In a majority of the cases I have found that a person who has become irresponsible may suffer frustration or back problems and a person who has committed fraud or who has accused others falsely may suffer acne problems.

You may call it karma or action and reaction, but further research will show that yogis and saints were not affected in the ancient days by health problems because of their purity in action.

What we eat, drink and wear, and how we sleep have a lot to do with our health and enjoyment of the world. You may be a millionaire or the richest tycoon, but if you are not in good health, the wealth is useless to you if you do no eat properly. Because our body is made up of the same proteins as red meat as in beef, pork, duck, goat, deer, etc., these meats are not easily digested and will cause a tremendous amount of health problems, such as brain tumors, poisonous blood, cancer, etc. Red meats should be avoided if you desire perfect health.

Alcohol, cigarettes and processed drugs cause impurities in our blood and fluid systems of our body and therefore should be avoided or should be taken in moderation. Our body functions and grows as a result of sunlight, which contains nine forms of electromagnetic energy that is necessary for the working of our body's electrical system. That system can break down or slow down due to shortages of vitamin D and other sunlight energies. As a result of this we should avoid wearing black clothing or underwear since the black fabric will absorb all these good light energies from our body. It has been found that black clothing causes the body's main electrical conduit – the spinal cord – to create back pain and headaches when its energy is low.

In an electrical generator, the construction for producing electricity requires that there must be both north and south pole magnets. In between those two, a conductor is aligned in an east-west direction. This contraption produces electrical energy in the conductor from which we can trap such energy to light our homes and so on. Well, the Earth has a North Pole and a South Pole that forms magnetic energy around us that keeps our human body energized.

However, to really take advantage of this energy in a harmonious way, it is advisable that we become like the conductor in the generator and align our bodies in an east-west direction in our beds when we are sleeping. This way we will energize our bodies to the extent of having no health problems. If you try this yourself, you will notice that you will not get up out of bed angry or weak in the morning.

In the following pages, I attempt to tell you the diseases and health problems you *could* have if your life is negative and unharmonious with your environment. My advice to you is to follow all the laws of nature and to accept all things as they are and not how you would like them to be.

In the following paragraphs, you will find the information that applies to you according to your Vedic Birth Code as found on Table 6.1 in Chapter 6.

Vedic Health Code for Birth Code #1
Nervousness caused by worrying
Mental problems as a result of loneliness and
    childhood abuse
Possible depression that can lead to insanity and cruelty
Spinal cord problems and brain tumor problems

Vedic Health Code for Birth Code #2
Dental problems
Diabetes, heart problems, dark spots (knees)
Blood pressure and breathing problems
Food poisoning problems

Vedic Health Code for Birth Code #3
Menstrual cycle problems
Excessive bleeding, back/head ache
Miscarriages and still born infants
Infertility and temper tantrums
Sexual diseases and problems

Vedic Health Code for Birth Code #4
Stress from hard work
Obesity as a result of laziness
Heart problems, hyper tension
Bone problems and stomach problems
Indigestion and weaknesses

Vedic Health Code for Birth Code #5
Sexual problems, eye problems, headache, nervousness
Feet problems, skin problems

Blood poisoning and muscle problems
Kidney and bladder problems

Vedic Health Code for Birth Code #6
Accidents and surgery
Broken bones, back pain, migraine headaches
Cancer, hypertension, heart attacks and many other
    ailments
You are accident-prone and may suffer from falls.

Vedic Health Code for Birth Code #7
Heart problems, addiction to drugs and alcohol
Insanity, possession by spirits and physical disabilities
Children may be born retarded or disabled.
Can be given false medicine by doctors

Vedic Health Code for Birth Code #8
Constipation problems
Obesity, nervousness, heart attacks
Anorexia and inferiority, complex about looks and
    appearance
Weakness to sunlight and eye problems

Vedic Health Code for Birth Code #9
General health is weak
Hyper-pressure, diabetes, heart problems, accidental
    death
Surgery
These people are affected by all kinds of health
    problems and should be very careful about their
    actions in life with regard to what they eat and with
    whom they come into contact.
Most people in this category suffer from alcoholic and
    drug problems
To maintain a generally good health pattern you are
    advised to take baths in the ocean regularly and to
    eat mostly a seafood diet.

Chapter 23

The Travel Code

When we travel we move from one set of space to another set of space in the Universe. As we travel we replace the energy that was in the space previous to the one that we are presently occupying. Sometimes we can move into a positive space or a negative one, and our own energy can conflict with that location or space. Difficulties in travel can occur when we enter a space that conflicts with our own. It is almost similar to the motion of moving from one home to the next where the number of the house is an identifying factor that can determine whether the house or home will conflict with us or not, as shown in Chapter 12, where we discussed the Location Code. When you enter a vehicle or an airplane or simply leave your front door and venture onto the road, you experience a *change of space*, which creates a new path or journey.

If we wish to determine whether it is a good time to travel or whether our trip or journey will be successful, or whether we will be traveling safely without any obstacles then we have to use the Vedic Travel Code as a guide. The factors involved in determining this code are:

The direction of your travel.
The day you are traveling.
The time that you leave home.

The Eastern direction is known as the most auspicious and lucky direction, so also the Western direction. Traveling in the North direction is fairly safe. However, sudden direction travel paths are somewhat troublesome and obstacles.

To find a proper time for traveling you must be able to use the table below. The table is divided into Vedic Birth

Codes on the left columns and days of the month on the top row. To find your good or bad day for traveling, look or the day of the month when you plan to travel and cross it with the number next in line with your Vedic Birth Code.

For example, if your Vedic Birth Code is #5 and you're traveling on the 1st of the month or the 10th of the month, the Vedic Travel Code will be #6. Now look up the meaning of the #6 Travel Code in the paragraphs that follow Table 23.1. You may notice that such a day may be negative for traveling. You can either try to change the date to a positive one or at least plan to expect many delays, frustration and tedious moments during your travel, so prepare to leave early and pray that you avoid any serious mishaps.

TABLE 23:1 - VEDIC TRAVEL CODES								
DAY OF THE MONTH YOU ARE TRAVELLING								
YOUR VEDIC BIRTH CODE	1 10 19 28	2 11 20 29	3 12 21 30	4 13 22 31	5 14 23	6 15 24	7 16 25	8 17 26	9 18 27
1	2	3	4	5	6	7	8	9	1
2	3	4	5	6	7	8	9	1	2
3	4	5	6	7	8	9	1	2	3
4	5	6	7	8	9	1	2	3	4
5	6	7	8	9	1	2	3	4	5
6	7	8	9	1	2	3	4	5	6
7	8	9	1	2	3	4	5	6	7
8	9	1	2	3	4	5	6	7	8
9	1	2	3	4	5	6	7	8	9

Vedic Travel Code # 1

A *fair* day for traveling.

Most likely you'll be traveling alone.

You'll have lots of time to think and meditate.
You may spend most of your time worrying about
things in your life.
Take a book, you may need it while traveling.

Vedic Travel Code # 2
An *excellent* day for traveling.
You may be traveling with a partner or family.
You will enjoy the company that you are traveling with.
Prepare to be talking or listening to music with someone.
Dress well as you may be meeting people on your trip.

Vedic Travel Code # 3
An *excellent* day for traveling.
You may be traveling with children or young people.
This may be an educational trip to a seminar or school
project.
You may be watching a lot of television or
entertainment media.
Take a notepad and book as you may be spending time
writing or reading.
Prepare to go to a party or social event on this trip.

Vedic Travel Code # 4
A *negative* day for traveling.
A hard and stressful day lies ahead.
This trip may be job related or a business trip.
If not job related, prepare to be tired at the end of your
trip.
You may be carrying extra luggage today.
Make sure you take extra lunch and snacks as you
may need them.
Try to rest as much as you can after this trip.

Vedic Travel Code # 5
An *excellent* day for traveling.
This will be a fun trip or a vacation journey.

Whether you're traveling alone or with others you will
   enjoy yourself.
This may be a long distance trip or one out of state or
   country.
You will return from this trip very satisfied and
   rejuvenated.
Be careful of fraudulent contacts and deceptive agents.

Vedic Travel Code # 6

A *negative* day for traveling.
Whichever way you look at it, the trip ahead is rough.
You may experience delays, additional costs and losses.
Be careful of accidents if you're driving or of thieves if
   you're shopping.
Prepare to leave home early so as to avoid delays.
You may get frustrated and angry during the trip.
A good advice is to accept all delays without arguments
   as this may be in your best interest; acceptance
   may save you from disaster.
If you're visiting your family, prepare to have family
   disagreements after your trip
Try to change your date to a good day for travel; it will
   help.

Vedic Travel Code # 7

A *fair* day for traveling.
Nothing exciting or interesting will happen on this trip.
You will be doing a lot of inner analysis of yourself and
   your life.
Take time off to meditate and plan your future well.
Avoid getting drunk or intoxicated on this trip.
You may encounter religious individuals or astrologers.
Prepare to fall asleep sometime on your journey.
Enjoy this quiet moment by yourself; you will feel
   rested at the end.

Vedic Travel Code # 8

An *excellent* day for traveling.

If this is not a business trip, it must be for pleasure indeed.

Prepare to spend lots of money on this trip.

If you're visiting casinos or gambling you may win.

You may encounter beautiful and handsome individuals in your journey.

Prepare to watch TV, look at fashions or enjoy great scenery.

Business meetings and partnerships will be successful on this trip.

Prepare to bring back lots of good stuff when you return.

Vedic Travel Code # 9

A *negative* day for traveling.

Whichever way you look at it, the trip ahead is rough.

You may experience delays, additional costs, and losses.

Be careful of accidents if you're driving or of thieves if you're shopping.

This could be a journey to a funeral or hospital or a court.

If you're traveling to a government center, prepare for delays.

If your trip is changed without your control, do not protest as it may be for your own good.

The location that you are leaving will demand you return to it soon.

You may definitely have baggage problems, and additional expenses, so make sure you walk with extra money.

I hope that the above travel codes will guide you to make travel plans that will take you and bring you back safe from your journeys. Vedic Code of Science is recognized for its potential in preventing unfortunate and lucky occurrences in a person's life. Armed with the knowledge of this science, people can learn to travel safely.

Chapter 24

The Depression Code

The human body is unique in its fingerprints and in its voiceprint, and each of us is different in appearance from other human beings. Our bodies inside contain energy sensors called *Chakras*. Each Chakra is like a generator that produces a unique feeling or emotion of its own in the body of that individual. These Chakras are like energy generators along our spinal column. There are nine Chakra generators within our spine stretching from the private area going upward all the way to the top of the brain forming the shape of a serpent. Sometimes this Chakra system is referred to as the "serpent energy" within us that creates our desires, feelings, emotions and, most important of all, our egos.

The following is a list of each Chakra and the areas of life that are controlled by that Chakra:

TABLE 24:1-CODES FOR CHAKRA ENERGY POINTS IN OUR BODY			
CHAKRA NUMBER	CHAKRA LOCATION	CHAKRA EFFECT	AREA OF LIFE THAT IS CONTROLLED BY THAT CHAKRA ENERGY
1	Base of the Spine	Sexuality	Partnerships & Sexuality
2	Below the Belly	Birth	Birth and relationship to Children
3	inside the Navel	Relations	All of our social life and Family
4	Stomach Area	Digestion	What you eat and response to food
5	Heart Area	Love Life	Feelings for others, Our Emotions

TABLE 24:1-CODES FOR CHAKRA ENERGY POINTS IN OUR BODY			
CHAKRA NUMBER	CHAKRA LOCATION	CHAKRA EFFECT	AREA OF LIFE THAT IS CONTROLLED BY THAT CHAKRA ENERGY
6	Speech Area	Mantra	What we say to create our karmas
7	Eye & Forehead	Visions	Our visions of others and how we see things
8	Brain Area	Intelligence	Our Knowledge and our Expectations
9	The Subtle Body	The Soul	The Control we have over our Destiny

At the time of birth, this Chakra system is usually very dormant and is coiled like a spring at the base of the spine. As the baby grows and learns to walk, the first and second Chakra begins its journey upwards, like a serpent. As the head of the coiled serpent reaches the third Chakra, it begins to identify its place in society. When the baby has reached the ninth Chakra, around age 10, the period of adolescence starts to influence the child and so the sexual Chakra begins to open up and the growing child identifies sexual orientation.

If the child is abused at any point between age 5 to age 13 the "coiled serpent energy" rapidly moves upward without control and a tremendous amount of energy is poured out into the sexual Chakra system. When this happens, the now sexually obsessed person will start to orient his sexuality in an abnormal and deformed way. Because of the inability of the young child to understand the massive confusion occurring within its own body and the enormous sexual energy being poured into the spinal column, he/she may seek out members of the same sex as partners (referred to as homosexuality). If he is unable to find a partner, he may become depressed and this may lead to suicidal tendencies.

If the individual is able to survive a molested or abusive childhood, this feeling of being subdued forcibly will be carried into the love connection where it will create tremendous love connection problems. This may result in violent love connections or divorces. The Vedic Code of Science has provided certain remedies that may help people to understand what has happened to them and what methods they should employ to cure this problem.

A curing of this problem will result in happiness in love connection life thus minimizing the divorce and separation occurring between married couples. If no curing occurs, then the maladies of impotence, menstrual cramps, infertility, lack of love and sex among the couples, and many more that will result in depression. Modern doctors have not provided any real cure for depression, but rather have divided temporary relief in the form of tranquilizers and anti-depressants.

In the following paragraphs, we are going to provide some natural and effective suggestions for curing depressions according to your Vedic Birth Code.

Vedic Birth Code #1 – Cure for Depression
Your depression is linked to loneliness and rejection.
You feel that no one cares about you and you are all alone.
- To cure this you need to meditate and pray, avoid too much drugs
- Find things to do on your own, projects that you will that will make you feel accomplished.

It's possible you were abused at a young age;
    forgiveness is very important.
Being a supervisor or boss makes you feel good in your
    life.

Vedic Birth Code #2 – Cure for Depression
Your depression concerns your love life and gossip.
You feel there is not enough love in you life.

You get depressed when some one criticizes you negatively.

If you are unable to find love or perform sexually you will be depressed.

Watch what you say as this will help to cure your depression.

Show your dedication by being subservient and you will receive attention.

Cooperate with others always and offer to help; it will cure your depression.

Pray that nobody takes advantage of your good heart... learn cooking lessons.

Vedic Birth Code #3 – Cure for Depression

Your depression concerns children and control.

You hate when you people do not listen or pay attention to you.

Loss of a child or worrying about pregnancy depresses you.

Reading, playing with children, babysitting or watching movies cures your depression.

Accept the fact that you cannot get everyone to listen to you and take up writing, teaching or reading as a hobby.

Having a baby cures your depressive moments.

Vedic Birth Code #4 – Cure for Depression

Your depression is about job, career advancement and hard work.

You think always that you are working too hard for too little pay.

You tend to be stressed out and have problems with co-workers.

Accept that jealousy from others is a good thing since it indicates that you are progressing in life.

Perform your duties without question and you will get rewarded eventually.

Try to relax and take a nap in the afternoon every day; it will help you.

Vedic Birth Code #5 – Cure for Depression

Your depression is about the opposite sex, freedom to do things and being bored easily.

Sometimes you think God is not watching so you try to break the rules of life.

The result can land you in jail, trouble with family and denial of love from others.

You worry about your sexual strength...you get depressed if impotent or frigid.

If your freedom is restricted you get depressed, so avoid such situations.

It's possible you were sexually abused as a child; seek counseling on this.

Reading, traveling, writing, going to movies, and joining clubs will help to cure your depression. Keeping yourself busy helping others will bring joy to your life.

Vedic Birth Code #6 – Cure for Depression

Your depression will be about family, your power, and your fears about separation and your status or position in life.

You always have a fear of losing control to others and you fear the mysterious.

It depresses you if your family rejects you or if you are losing in career or school.

You like to be praised for your achievements; you hate changes in relationships.

Realize that you can't control the Universe; it has laws which control you.

Learn to bow and accept rules; before correcting others, correct yourself.

Accept all responsibility given to you; learn to gain from each experience.

You can become a great doctor, editor, lawyer or
   political leader...go for it!

Learn to spend time and buy gifts for the family; it will
   cure your depression.

Vedic Birth Code #7 – Cure for Depression

Your depression will be about your love life and your
   partner; avoid trouble by what you say and your
   connection with God or the Universe.

You keep most of your feelings inside so this will
   increase your depression.

Learn to speak out your feelings and express yourself
   outwardly.

Becoming a radio announcer, a DJ or public speaker
   will help you.

Addiction to alcohol and drugs will increase your
   depression.

Whenever you are depressed you try to get intoxicated;
   avoid drugs.

Vedic Birth Code #8 – Cure for Depression

Money, business, investments and lack of comfort
   depress you.

You worry about your money, your assets and your
   appearance.

You worry if your body is out of shape or if you are
   overweight.

Joining the gym or exercise classes will help to cure
   your depression.

You buy expensive things to impress the opposite sex;
   it's OK, go ahead.

Acting in movies, taking up yoga or making profit in a
   business is good for you.

Dressing up and pampering yourself with dining out
   and enjoying luxury satisfies your ego.

Vedic Birth Code #9 – Cure for Depression

You are very susceptible to depression and are
  confused a great deal.

You change your mind rapidly and can make those
  around you very confused.

Because of your constant doubts and denial of things,
  you create your own depressive moments; try to
  accept all things as they are.

Because money spends constantly in your hand you
  get broke easily; avoid impulsive buying.

You struggle for everything in life because of your
  suspicion of others; you must learn to listen to loved
  ones and trust them.

You must learn to bow to a higher power and become a
  student first before you can tell others what to do.

You try to create exciting moments by accusing others
  in a sly way; prepare for the backlash.

Bathing in the sea regularly and spending time at the
  beach will help you a great deal.

Chapter 25

The Vedic Career Code

According to the Vedic Code of Science, we are all born under a code called the Duty Code. The Duty Code refers to the fact that each one of us has our own duty towards the Universe. For example, the duty of the bee is to pollinate the flowers and the duty of plants is to provide oxygen.

Each one of us also has our career or job to make the Universe around us function and progress. We are made to fulfill a duty that will contribute towards the continuity of the Universe. Without work, the Universe cannot function.

Each element in the Universe is working constantly to keep the Universe alive. When we are given a job to do it is because that job was attracted to us through karma that was performed by our parents, grandparents and ancestors. For example, if you find your father or mother was involved in real estate sales at the time of your birth, then you also will be attracted to this type of career or job. If your father was a farmer at the time of your birth, you will possess an unconscious knowledge of farming.

Everything that happens to us between the age of 0 and 7 determines what type of career we will follow. A good look at the Hereditary Code (Chapter 9) may also indicate some of the characteristics that we learn from our parents at the time of pregnancy that will contribute to our choice of career. This factor and the other fact that our father or mother might have been involved in a particular type of career will influence our abilities and skills in the kind of career we will follow in our own life.

There are 9 main categories of career classification in the Universe. These are referred to as Vedic Career Codes, and they are as follows:

TABLE 25:1 - CAREER CODES

CAREER TYPE OR CATEGORY	VD CD	CAREER TYPE OR CATEGORY	VD CD
Airlines, Automobiles, Trucking	5	Janitor & Maintenance Workers	9
Architecture, Printing	3	Jewelry & Gem Stone Services	8
Art, Editing	6	Judges & Court Reporting Services	9
Astrology, Writing	3	Landlord & Tenants	4
Babysitting, Toys	3	Lawyers, Police Officers	6
Banking, Check Cashing Services	4	Legal & Court Services	9
Building, Carpentry, Contracting	4	Managers, Supervisors, Foremen	1
Chefs, Cooks	2	Medical Doctors, Pharmaceuticals	7
Child Care, Pediatrics	3	Merchants & Businessmen	8
Congress, Senate Leaders	6	Messengers & Postal Services	5
Consulting, Science	5	Modeling & Fashion Designing Industry	8
Creative Writing, Community Leaders	1	Mortgages & Loans	6
Criminal Justice, Prison Services	9	Acting & Producing	8
Critics, Secret Agents	7	Nursing & Care-giving Services	2
Drugs and Alcohol Services	7	Politics, Government	6
Email, Internet Service Providers	5	Publishing & Communication	3
Entrepreneurs, Investors	8	Real Estate, Farming	4
Fabrics and Clothes Manufacturing	4	Religious Advisors, Spiritual Counselors	7
Family Court, Divorce Consultants	6	Revenue & Tax Collection	4
Farming, Agriculture	4	Salesmen & Store Owners	8

TABLE 25:1 - CAREER CODES			
CAREER TYPE OR CATEGORY	VD CD	CAREER TYPE OR CATEGORY	VD CD
Filming & Videotaping Services	8	Stock Market, Securities, Brokerage Service	4
Firefighters & Military Personnel	6	Teachers & Educators	3
Food & Restaurant Industry	2	Television and Theatre	3
Funeral & Burial Services	9	Transportation & Travel Industry	5
Vacationing, Moving Companies	5	Yoga & Exercising	3

As you can see from Table 25.1, each of us is born with certain skills suitable for a specific job or career. If you find that the career you have presently is not satisfactory in any way, you should work with the list on Table 25.1 and change into the appropriate career or job. Getting raises and promotions in a job depends on how you perform and how dedicated you are with the job. However, the following Career Analysis Table will provide the Code for how well you do with the job or career that you now have.

Follow the top row to find your Vedic Birth Code as shown in Chapter 6, then follow the left row to find your Vedic Career Code from the paragraphs above, then cross the two to find your Vedic Job Status Code. For example, if you are in the real estate, your Vedic Career Code is #4 and if your Vedic Birth Code is #5 then your Vedic Job Status Code is #9 on Table 25.2. After that, find the interpretations of your Vedic Job Status Code in the paragraphs that follow.

TABLE 25:2 - VEDIC JOB STATUS CODES									
CAREER CODE #	YOUR VEDIC BIRTH CODE								
	1	**2**	**3**	**4**	**5**	**6**	**7**	**8**	**9**
#1	2	3	4	5	6	7	8	9	1
#2	3	4	5	6	7	8	9	1	2
#3	4	5	6	7	8	9	1	2	3
#4	5	6	7	8	9	1	2	3	4
#5	6	7	8	9	1	2	3	4	5
#6	7	8	9	1	2	3	4	5	6
#7	8	9	1	2	3	4	5	6	7
#8	9	1	2	3	4	5	6	7	8
#9	1	2	3	4	5	6	7	8	9

Vedic Job Status Code #1

Good, full of pressures and opportunities to get promoted

May be promoted rapidly upward

Will be given a lot of responsibility and leadership position

Always will be asked to assist management

This job will be good if you like to teach and lead others.

Vedic Job Status Code #2

Your co-workers and managers will be excellent and cooperative.

You will be liked favored by your managers and supervisors.

You will be known as a dutiful and dedicated employee.

You will feel comfortable with this job.

Vedic Job Status Code #3

Many excellent and good opportunities for advancement

Everyone will have a good sense of humor at the workplace.

You'll find comfort in this job as a learning experience.
This job may involve further training and knowledge.
You'll get many raises and help.
If in the media business you may travel a great deal.

Vedic Job Status Code #4

A fair and hard working job with average pay.
You could experience a lot of stress with this job.
You will be constantly busy and always doing
    something.
You may be working a lot of overtime on this job.
The raises will come to you slowly but they will be
    good.
Try to rest and eat properly while working this job.

Vedic Job Status Code #5

You will experience constant changes and movement
    with this job.
Your duties will be changed often by your bosses.
Will be promoted and given raises often
Learn to accept changes without question and your
    bosses will like you.
This job may involve traveling, if so, do it.
At this job you may be tempted to take home things
    from your workplace; try to avoid it.
If you're a female you may experience sexual
    harassment by bosses.

Vedic Job Status Code #6

You will find this job frustrating and full of
    responsibilities.
There will be a fight for power between you and your
    co-workers.
There will be many disagreements between you and
    the people of authority.
Avoid participating with other coworkers in stealing or
    robbing the company.

If this is a partnership, it will incur in serious disaster before being separated.

Be careful of injuries or accidents on this job; your back may affect you while working.

The best way to make this job positive is to perform all your duties with full dedication and learn to bow mentally to those in power.

Vedic Job Status Code #7

Your work progress and promotions will be very slow on this job.

Very few people will bother you on this job.

If you start to move upward there will be jealousies by coworkers.

You will be left alone to work by yourself most of the time.

This job could require you to do a lot of analysis.

Try to maintain a proper diet, as you may feel sleepy during working hours.

Take time off to meditate sometimes.

Vedic Job Status Code #8

Your place of work will be very extravagant and comforting.

This job may involve the handling in lots of money or finance.

The people around you will always be dressed richly in appearance.

This job may involve a lot of people with ego.

There will be a battle for power and money among the workers.

You will receive constant raises and promotions at this job.

If you're a female you may experience sexual harassment by bosses.

To enjoy this job, help your employer make and save money.

Vedic Job Status Code #9

Low pay, lots of tension and dissatisfaction will be the
effect of this job.

You constantly complain about the pay not being
enough for the work.

You may get into trouble because of confusion with
orders and duties.

You imagine that others do not like you; avoid this
negativity.

Be careful of injury, sickness or danger on this job.

Someone with high ego may constantly harass you at
this job.

Raises are scarce but when you get them, keep quiet.

Keep a low profile and avoid arguments and then you
will be able to enjoy this job for a long time.

Chapter 26

The Money Code

Money makes the world go round, as some people may say. The Vedic Code of Science recognizes money as a force that creates continuity of the Universe. In this science, money is considered to be a direct link to the power of light. Without light, there is no appearance of materiality. For something to have value it must have existence and, so, therefore if there is a lack of light there is a lack of wealth.

For example, imagine if the Sun did not rise for one day. No one would be able to wake up to a fully material world and since there would be no light, no business trading or selling of goods could take place. How many of you realize that our whole concept of wealth depends upon your daily activities according to the Sunlight?

Besides controlling our wealth, the Sun contributes to the growth of all things that we eat as well as use for our comfort; hence, as you can see the Sun controls our health as well.

There is an old saying "Money grows on trees." You will be amazed that this old saying may be true after all. Only members of the plant kingdom provide foods to all animals and humans. Whatever we cook and eat is as a result of the growth of plants, trees and herbs. Whether it is the fruits from the trees, the roots or the leaves, they become our source of energy directly or indirectly! After eating our food, we obtain enough energy to work and earn money, which then we use to pay our bills and buy all things we desire. So it is safe to say that, "Money does come from trees."

Like all things, money should be respected and treated as a divine energy that is used by all of us to enjoy this world. There are nine forms of money energy, which affect all of us according to our actions in life. For example, you may notice that if we fail to perform our duties properly to our employers, we will be denied raises. Or another example is if we steal money from others, we will lose our wealth in many different ways.

The nine forms of money are:

Creativity – money affecting the mind and desire

Sharing – money affecting relationship with others

Knowledge – money affecting children, education and comfort

Duty – money affecting your job and your foundation

Movement – money for pleasure and changes

Power – money affecting your status and your responsibilities

Emotion – money affecting your spiritual relationship with the Universe

Enjoyment – money that makes you enjoy power, luxury and beauty

Health – money affecting the condition of your life with regard to diseases, confinement and karma

TABLE 26:1 YOUR MONEY CODES

VEDIC BIRTH CODE	VEDIC MONEY CODE	VEDIC BIRTH CODE	VEDIC MONEY CODE
1	9	6	5
2	1	7	6
3	2	8	7
4	3	9	8
5	4		

Vedic Money Code #1

You worry about money too much.

Whenever you have too much money you feel you have power.

Not having money makes you feel too dependent on others.

Loss of money can cause you to be depressed.

Avoid gambling, as you can become addicted to it.

Too much greed for money can make you very abusive and very insulting.

Think of your bills and pay them before pleasure.

Vedic Money Code #2

You love to look for bargains and save money in shopping.

You purchase items that are sometimes useless to you.

Most of your money is spent on jewelry, clothes, and decorating the home.

You have a secret stash of cash hidden away for hard times.

Spending money on food or restaurants will be beneficial.

You usually have money at all times.

You like to spend your money to buy gifts for others.

You cannot own your own business because you give away too much.

Vedic Money Code #3

You dream of winning the lottery or jackpot; it could happen.

You like to use money to buy toys and childish items.

You use money as an opportunity to attract the attention of others.

You may earn lots of money as teachers, actors and models.

Money can create quarrels between you, your friends and lovers.

Money used for books or readings will benefit you.

Vedic Money Code #4

You have to work hard for your money.

Most of your money coming in you will eventually spend out again.

Sometimes you have to go through much sacrifice to make money.

Lack of money causes you stress and depression.

Avoid borrowing money, as it can be hard to pay back.

Raises and promotions will be slow coming at work.

Save as much as you can – bigger savings make you feel secure.

Vedic Money Code #5

Money moves rapidly in your life.

You'll make an excellent businessperson, as you're skilled in sales.

Because of your skills with words, you can sell anything to anyone.

A lot of your money is spent on cars, airlines, and traveling.

You spend lots of money on pleasure and comfort.

Females spend money mostly on fashion and gyms for exercise.

You change your mind quickly when trying to purchase something for others.

You may have problems with the revenue department – be honest with taxes.

Avoid fraud, deception and robbery of others and money will love to be with you.

Vedic Money Code #6

Lack of money makes you very frustrated and irresponsible.

You must be careful, as credit card debt will become high.

You love to borrow money and to take loans from the bank.

Credit and owing others can be your downfall.

You become angry and critical if someone owes you money.

You look upon money as a power of influence and politics.

You could end up paying lots of taxes and fees to court of government.

You could lose money by robbery, thieves or fraudulent partners.

Vedic Money Code #7

You're very secretive about money.

Even though money may not be important to you, you need it.

You spend lots of money on your parents.

Using money for real estate is lucky for you.

You do not like when other people owe you money.

You become very emotional about your savings and your earnings.

Raises and bonuses come to you slowly but surely.

You do well in business money wise.

You may secretly spend or earn money from bars or clubhouses.

Very few people know about your finance.

You are lucky with the stock market and any farming business.

Vedic Money Code #8

You like to spend money on quality and expensive things.

Your extravagant taste makes you spend lots of money.

Money passes through your hands very easily.

Sometimes you spend money without worrying about other priorities.

Many of you become models, fashion designers, actors or investors.

Having a business of your own makes you earn a great deal of money.

When you have a lot of money, you seek too much pleasure with the opposite sex, which eventually creates your downfall.

Excessive abuse of power because of money can land you in jail.

Vedic Money Code #9

Definitely a difficult money path is laid out for you in this life.

You struggle to earn every dime in your life – learn to save.

You'll be very fickle in your spending habits.

Be careful of robbery or conflicts with others about money.

Negative in your attitude towards money causes you to suffer court fines, medical costs, loss of savings and bankruptcy.

Money kept in your hand is spent very easily.

It seems you're always spending money to do all kinds of things without thinking of saving your money for hard times.

Giving to charity as well as doing services for the poor helps you to generate lots of money; participating in temple activities benefits you.

Working with the government relieves you of negative money problems.

Chapter 27

The Investment Code

When people invest in a home – the American dream – the stock market or in a business of their own, and then surprisingly lose it in a few months or a few years, they and their friends often wonder what caused such a loss. Most of the time it is due to lack of knowledge of business strategies or the timing of when the investment was made. [As far as timing of investments goes, I will discuss that in Volume 2 of this series.]

What you need to know now is whether you will be successful in any particular type of investments and what investments are good for you. When you invest in a certain type of investment, your chances of gaining a profit may be greater than in certain other types. The most important factors that govern any investment are type, timing and matching with karmic Codes of Life. As Shakespeare said: "Some are born great. Some achieve greatness. And some have greatness thrust upon them."

Before proceeding to find out about the effect of your Vedic Investment Code, you must first read the chapter on the Vedic Money Code (Chapter 26), so you'll have a better understanding as to how your Vedic Investment Code will affect you.

Not everyone is suitable for certain types of investments; so knowing what types of investments are suitable for you increases your chances of making profits and becoming wealthy. On the Table 27.1, I have selected the most popular types of investments that can be compared to your Vedic Birth Code to help you understand the best types of investments that you can get into. However, it doesn't mean you should shut out other investments completely. Perhaps a partner, who is compatible with you, would be able to work with certain investments that are negative with your birth code but positive with your partner's.

In the following table you will find a selected set of investment categories that matches your Vedic Birth Code. Following Table 27.1 are the interpretations of the Vedic Investment Code in combination with the investment type of your Vedic Birth Code.

TABLE 27:1 - VEDIC INVESTMENT CODES									
INVESTMENT TYPE	YOUR VEDIC BIRTH CODE								
	1	2	3	4	5	6	7	8	9
STOCK MARKET	5	6	7	8	9	1	2	3	4
MONEY	9	1	2	3	4	5	6	7	8
SAVINGS BANK	5	6	7	8	9	1	2	3	4
LAND	5	6	7	8	9	1	2	3	4
GAMBLING	9	1	2	3	4	5	6	7	8
MOVIES	4	5	6	7	8	9	1	2	3
PUBLISHING	4	5	6	7	8	9	1	2	3
JEWELRY	9	1	2	3	4	5	6	7	8
FARMING	5	2	3	4	5	6	7	8	9
REAL ESTATE	5	6	7	8	9	1	2	3	4
CONSTRUCTION	5	6	7	8	9	1	2	3	4
ROMANCE	3	4	5	6	7	8	9	1	2
IMPORT/EXPORT	6	7	8	9	1	2	3	4	5

Check the Vedic Investment Code above and read below the Vedic Code that matches it.

Vedic Investment Code #1
You have to do it all by yourself – having a partner is trouble.
To make this investment profitable you need to maintain and research all information about it.
Try to seek leadership and creativity in this investment, as this helps you improve profits.
Avoid becoming too dominant.

Vedic Investment Code #2

A good business doing partner ship with spouse, friend or family member

You always make profits as long as your relationship with the people involved is positive.

Learn to be very cooperative with the people you meet in this investment and watch what you say, as this can cause you losses.

Vedic Investment Code #3

Many opportunities present themselves in this business for you.

Always maintain constant knowledge about your investments, then your profits will always be high.

Try to maintain a good sense of humor as it brings profits.

Avoid childishness or immature controlling of others.

Vedic Investment Code #4

This investment requires that you work very hard.

No matter how hard you work, you have to work harder to make any profits with this investment.

Vedic Investment Code #5

A constant changing investment, which requires rapid thinking and action before you can become successful.

Constant change and new ideas are needed to make this investment profitable.

Watch out for fraudulent and deceptive people.

Vedic Investment Code #6

An investment that requires research, responsibility and power.

This investment should never have a partnership.

Avoid confrontation, conflicts and disagreements in this investment as you may lose your investment.

Watch out for thieves and robbers.

Vedic Investment Code #7

This investment must be done with the utmost discretion and secrecy.

All transactions in this investment should be done with caution, and profits will come to you slowly but surely.

Research into the background of this investment, as there may be secret pitfalls awaiting you.

Vedic Investment Code #8

A very lucrative and profitable investment.

Invest as much as you can and with good timing your sales will become profitable.

Most of the people you contact regarding this investment will want to be paid their fair share.

Vedic Investment Code #9

You should avoid this type of investment.

Extreme caution is needed with his investment or else you will lose a great deal of money.

Try to invest as little as you can and do not spend too much money on improvements, as this will create very little profit.

Buying and selling quickly is better as a short term investment.

Consult with a priest regarding your investment.

Chapter 28

The War Code

The Vedic Code of Science recognizes that war occurs within the relationships of all living and nonliving things. War creates termination and renewal within the Universe. Don't get me wrong; I'm not trying to say war is a good thing. As you read before in the Chapter of the Disaster Code, I emphasized the fact that the disaster created in the Universe is referred to as an act of God (as quoted in our insurance polices), whereas war is a destructive situation created by human or the organism itself. Within the Vedic Code of War we have to consider the fact that there must be enmity, animosity, jealousy, hatred and competition between rivals that is created prior to the actual occurrence of a war. These very qualities mentioned are referred to as "negative" actions that create bad karma. Therefore we have to conclude that war is a result of karma.

In the Vedic Code of Science, the Vedic War Code is indicated by the #6. The Vedic #6, when placed in its multiplicity (6 x 6 + 36) that reaches the Vedic Code #9, usually results in deadly wars. An observation of the ninth letter of the English alphabet, which is letter "I," will reveal that this letter is associated with distress, death and destruction. Please note also that the Vedic Code #9 is a reversed position of the Vedic Code #6.

As you know, the Book of Revelations in the Bible refers to the number 666. When 6+6+6 is added together it equals 18, which is Vedic Code #9, and also letter "I." Let's take a look at the examples found in our Universe so far to reflect this theory.

Some of you may not have known this but a check of history books prove that the following countries were all involved in deadly wars in some point of history: India,

China, Iran, Iraq, Fiji, Indonesia, Lybia, Israel, Sri Lanka and many others. Please note that the first vowel in every one of these country names is an "I." It is also further noted that terrorism or holy wars, which is the result of egotistical behavior of the people, have affected these countries. Unlike the freedom and patriotic wars, such as the American War of Independence or the war for the Emancipation of Slavery, the wars in eastern countries were deadlier than ever.

Similarly, each individual person has an ego, which can be inflated to the point of creating such things like jealousy and enmity that can lead to war. So before we can proceed to interpret the Vedic War Code, we must first look at the Vedic Enemy Code between two individuals. Table 28.1 indicates the comparison between the Vedic Birth Code of a person listed at the top row and the Vedic Birth Code of another person on the left column. When crossing these two, the resulting number becomes the Vedic Enemy Code.

One of the most important things that we must realize is that jealousy can be a good thing or a bad thing. When a person is jealous of another person, it is an indication that the victim of the jealousy is really progressing in comparison to the aggressor, who may not be progressing. In other words, if you are the one receiving the jealousy from others, it is an indication that the person is jealous because you are progressing higher than they are. This is a good thing, as it indicates that you are doing well. However, sad to say, the people who may be jealous of you are suffering from the sickness of envy. When someone is envious of you, it means that they have too much ego thus this pride becomes their downfall. This jealous person has two choices: he can view you as the competition and try to strive higher or he can become negative and seek ways to bring about your downfall. If he chooses the latter then he may also bring about his own downfall.

TABLE 28:1 - VEDIC ENEMY/WAR CODES									
YOUR VEDIC BIRTH CODE	YOUR PARTNER'S VEDIC BIRTH CODE								
	1	*2*	*3*	*4*	*5*	*6*	*7*	*8*	*9*
1	2	3	4	5	6	7	8	9	1
2	3	4	5	6	7	8	9	1	2
3	4	5	6	7	8	9	1	2	3
4	5	6	7	8	9	1	2	3	4
5	6	7	8	9	1	2	3	4	5
6	7	8	9	1	2	3	4	5	6
7	8	9	1	2	3	4	5	6	7
8	9	1	2	3	4	5	6	7	8
9	1	2	3	4	5	6	7	8	9

Vedic Enemy Code #1

These two individuals will not become enemies, but rather they will become competitors.

They will always try to outdo the other person in everything.

Vedic Enemy Code #2

They will never become enemies; they will always be friends.

They will always love each other and consider one another's feelings.

The only war they will have will be a war for attention from each other.

Vedic Enemy Code #3

These two people are not enemies, but will have minor wars within their relationships.

Childish behavior or words can create enmity among these two.

There will be a battle for attention of other by both of the two.

Vedic Enemy Code #4

- These two will not become enemies unless the work together or live together.
- Friendship between these two without being attached to any material things will do well.
- There may be jealousy in the workplace that will be destructive.
- Coworkers may be competitive in their behavior for promotions.

Vedic Enemy Code #5

- Enmity is created in this relationship by distrust among these two.
- Both of these two people have a high degree of ego and pride.
- Neither of these two will admit that they're wrong, so that can create war.
- Sexuality may be a factor that creates enmity between these two.
- Each person wants to boss the other person around; this creates enmity.
- If one person restricts the other's freedom then there will be war.

Vedic Enemy Code #6

- There may be a dislike for each other from the time they meet.

There will be a fight for power between these two constantly.

They involve many others in their quarrel with each other.

War between these two people breaks out very often.

If these two cooperate they will become very powerful.

Neither of these two admits that the other is right.

They can become enemies and be at war all their lives.

Vedic Enemy Code #7

A relationship that very rarely creates war unless there is extreme jealousy for each other.

These two can be great religious and spiritual friends or extreme religious enemies.

The egos of both are high and they can hate to the point of destruction through jealousy.

Each person keeps their ill feelings of each other inside and then blows it all out one day creating war.

Each person is attached to the other emotionally; prayer can help avoid war.

Vedic Enemy Code #8

Money is the key factor that creates war between these two.

Power, investments, stock market, business and more are factors that cause war between these two.

Each person is competitive with the other in their achievements and watches each other carefully.

Each person wants to look better than the other looks.

Together if they cooperate they can make millions.

Vedic Enemy Code #9

A relationship that can surely lead to war and destruction.

Each person thinks and suspects the other of working against him or her.

There will be constant arguments and war even though they love each other a lot.

These two will end up in court surely if their fight becomes extreme with each other.

Money will be their destruction if loans are involved.

Each one creates confusion for the other person.

A third party is always required to settle the war between these two.

They are always denying their faults with each other.

Chapter 29

The Disaster Code

For change to happen, distress, chaos, upsets and upheavals must take place. It is a disaster that creates change from bad to good. Disasters create distress, which gives men or women the thought that life should not be taken for granted but that there are rules of the Universe, which cannot be broken.

Disaster is followed by renewal, and renewal creates continuity in the Universe: creation, presentation and destruction are the key elements of the Universe and these elements cause the Universe to exist. We all experience these elements of creation, presentation and destruction constantly in our lives. At one moment we experience new feelings, emotions and pleasures, and the next moment we experience destruction of those same things. In between these two that we try to preserve all that we acquire for as long as we can.

Our knowledge, actions and environmental connections determine how long we preserve the first experience. Knowledge can secure you if you know of the path toward destruction and can avoid it. Action (karma) can make you avoid the impending destruction and, if in the proper location or environment, the Universe will assist your preservation as long as you can uphold the first two.

For example, in one home on a street, there might be a person getting married, so everyone in that home is experiencing happiness, pleasure. Down the road not far away a person may have died by accident, and the people there are experiencing sadness and destruction of a life. As you can see, happiness and sadness can be on the same street.

Each person, city, state and country, and each animal and insect experiences creation, preservation and destruction.

At the time of writing of this chapter, Hurricane Wilma was about to hit the city of Cancun, Mexico and was headed for New Orleans and North Florida where it was expected to create more disaster. As I continued to write, CNN's Anderson Cooper was reporting that the 9th Ward of the City of New Orleans was still suffering from electricity blackout that resulted from Hurricane Katrina and Hurricane Rita.

I had sent a letter to CNN in August when Katrina struck New Orleans warning them that the levees were going to break again, and they replied saying that they did not think the information was important. The levees already broke twice. Please note that Hurricane Katrina struck New Orleans on the 28th of August (8+2+8 = 18 = 6+6+6) a Vedic Code #9 day. In addition to that New Orleans is a Vedic Birth Code of #1 and so is Biloxi, MS. When this Birth Code of #1 is added to the month of August the result is #9.

I have begun to observe a strange pattern in the location where all these disasters occur. It seems like the 9th letter of the English alphabet and the locations where disasters occur have a lot in common. Observe the following:

NAME	STORM	PLACES
Wilma	Hurricane	Cancun, Mexico
Katrina	Hurricane	Louisiana/MS
Rita	Hurricane	New Orleans/ TX
Ivan	Hurricane	Florida

Another interesting observation is the fact that wherever there are disasters, there is some form of evil corruption against the continuity of the Universe. In a way we can see that the Universe (or God) is fighting back by creating these disasters. Did you notice that the tsunami came right after some Muslim radicals were sacrificing hostages on TV, and then the tsunami also killed more than 25,000 Muslims? Did you notice also that New Orleans was a voodoo haven for the sacrifice of animals and sometimes humans? The movie "Skeleton's Key" was released by Hollywood at the time Katrina hit, and this movie is all about voodoo in New Orleans.

Take places like Iraq, Iran, Pakistan, Afghanistan and so on; you will observe that women there are disrespected and treated like dirt. In certain parts of India and China, girl babies are killed because a boy child is more favorable. Can you imagine the world existing without women? The Universe would die out eventually. Wherever there is respect for women, the location will progress. Without a woman, how can any man come?

War is founded in most eastern countries where women were once respected highly more than 500 years ago. These areas are where most terrorism takes place. Remember the 2nd Commandment about coveting your neighbor's land? This is what terrorism involves, the fighting for land, as in the Kashmir area where the earthquake killed more than 50,000 Muslims and 1300 Indians.

Hurricanes are good in one way and bad in another. Every time a hurricane damages an area, the building codes are revised and the new houses are built much improved and much stronger. Wherever an area is flooded, the land experiences a lot of sacrificial burial disguised as a form of religion. The tsunami occurred at Christmas time when people in the whole area were sacrificing the most animals for their holiday feast.

Take a look at the following facts and see what conclusions you can draw using the Vedic Code of Science. Notice the first vowel "I" in the names of the town, country or village.

DISASTER NAME	LOCATION OR PLACE	TYPE OF CORRUPTION
Earthquake	India	Sacrifice/Terrorism
Earthquake	Iran	Sacrifice/Terrorism
Earthquake	Islamabad	Sacrifice/Terrorism
Earthquake	Nicaragua	Drugs/Terrorism
Tsunami	Indonesia	Sacrifice/Terrorism
Tsunami	Sri Lanka	Sacrifice/Terrorism
Tsunami	India	Sacrifice/Terrorism
Tsunami	Fiji	Sacrifice/Terrorism
Tsunami	China	Communism/Terrorism
War	Iraq	Sacrifice /Terrorism
Floods	British Guyana	Sacrifice/Corruption

Now let us take a look at the dates of some of these disasters and you will observe some astonishing and interesting facts related to the number 666, the number of evil and destruction.

ELEMENT OF DISASTER	VEDIC CODE		BIRTH OF DISASTER
Wilma	9	10/17	Caribbean
Katrina	9	08/28	New Orleans
Rita	9	"r" is the 18th letter	
Earthquake	9	10/8	Pakistan/India
Earthquake	3+6	12/26/2004	Magnitude=9
Earthquake	9	1/26	India
Bombing	6	3/12	Spain subway

Chapter 30

The Vedic Car Code

The human body is a vehicle itself. It carries with it all the parts of the human body. A car can be compared to the human body the same way. It has a circulatory system, a brain, and eyes, which are the headlights. The horn is like the mouth; its fuel is like its stomach; and its wheels are its feet, and so on. You get the point! Therefore we should treat the car or vehicle as if it's another person or entity fetching us around in its belly.

Each car or vehicle has a Birth Code or Birth Identity, which in Vedic Science is known as the Vedic Car Code. This code identifies the vehicle by its year of origin and describes all the possible problems than can affect the car and gives the inner and outer strength of the vehicle itself. The following table will identify the Vedic Car Code by its year.

TABLE 30:1- YOUR CAR CODE

YEAR OF CAR MODEL	VEDIC CAR CODE	YEAR OF CAR MODEL	VEDIC CAR CODE
1982	2	1996	7
1983	3	1997	8
1984	4	1998	9
1985	5	1999	1
1986	6	2000	2
1987	7	2001	3
1988	8	2002	4
1989	9	2003	5
1990	1	2004	6
1991	2	2005	7

TABLE 30:1- YOUR CAR CODE				
YEAR OF CAR MODEL	VEDIC CAR CODE		YEAR OF CAR MODEL	VEDIC CAR CODE
1992	3		2006	8
1993	4		2007	9
1994	5		2008	1
1995	6		2009	2

Vedic Car Code #1 – All About Your Car

Good car, that will prove reliable

- Driving alone most of the time
- Problem starting sometimes or with lights and ignition area
- Usually has books and signs inside or outside the vehicle

Listens to talk shows while you drive.

Vedic Car Code #2 – All About Your Car

- This car will transport many people and will be used for shopping.

Always have music playing while you drive.

Romance, love and sex will be influenced by this car.

- The driver will always have company while driving.
- Problems in this car will be with seats, crowded trunk and problems with the inside of the car.

Front end problems

Vedic Car Code #3 – All About Your Car

Children will be part of this car's transport

This car will have an elaborate musical and speaker system

Most problems will be with the steering and guidance system.

Vedic Car Code #4 – All About Your Car

This car will be used primarily for job or career services.
A solid car and it could experience manufacturing
    problems.
The engine is stronger than the body of the car.

Vedic Car Code #5 – All About Your Car

This car accumulates a lot of mileage.
This car has wheel or transmission problems.
This car will change many hands quickly.
Usually a sports car, a race car or fast car.

Vedic Car Code #6 – All About Your Car

Lots of repairs and possible accident with this car.
Lots of traffic tickets.
You may experience loan payment problems with this
    car.
This car may have had an accident before you owned it
    and may be accident-prone.
Owner will spend lots of money on body repairs or
    exhaust system.

Vedic Car Code #7 – All About Your Car

There will be oil or water problems.
This car will be used for religious purposes.
• The owners are usually religious.
The driver will experience much thinking while driving
The atmosphere inside of the car will always be quiet
• If a negative person owns this car, he will be
  smoking or drinking alcohol or be addicted to
  something.
• Problems with this car may involve the controlling
  components of the engine.

Vedic Car Code #8 – All About Your Car

• A luxurious and expensive car.
• Most of these cars are custom made and rare.

- The driver experiences much comfort and may even have a chauffeur.
- The driver may also be a designer or model or actor in film or a businessman.

Vedic Car Code #9 – All About Your Car
- Water problems and possible radiator problems.
- Usually the first thing to go is the water pump or the fuel pump.
- Possible accident will damage the car but little injury to the driver.
- Owner will spend lots of money on repairs and maintenance.

Chapter 31

Your Vedic Transporter Code

Your Vedic Transporter Code is a combination of your Vedic Birth Code # and your Vedic Car Code #.

On Table 31.1 you will find a code matching your car, truck or van that acts as a protection for the human body as it moves in space. The human body is made to walk on Earth. When it is elevated off the Earth in a vehicle such as a plane, it must respond to the movements of that vehicle. The vehicle of course would respond with its own energy field together with the energy field of the human person. A measure of the resulted energy field would most likely tell how that car or vehicle would respond to your energy field when you are in it.

Table 31.1 tells you your Vedic Car Code and then gives an explanation for each code.

TABLE 31:1- VEDIC TRANSPORTER CODE									
YOUR VEDIC CAR CODES	Get Car Code # from Table 30:1 for the left column, follow row under your Vedic Birth Code Above to find the resulting Code								
	YOUR VEDIC BIRTH CODE								
	1	*2*	*3*	*4*	*5*	*6*	*7*	*8*	*9*
#1	2	3	4	5	6	7	8	9	1
#2	3	4	5	6	7	8	9	1	2
#3	4	5	6	7	8	9	1	2	3
#4	5	6	7	8	9	1	2	3	4
#5	6	7	8	9	1	2	3	4	5
#6	7	8	9	1	2	3	4	5	6
#7	8	9	1	2	3	4	5	6	7
#8	9	1	2	3	4	5	6	7	8
#9	1	2	3	4	5	6	7	8	9

Vedic Transporter Code #1
- Problems with accepting the car
- You will spend a lot of time driving this car alone.
- This car will hardly be driven on the road.
- You will worry about the payments on this car.
- All responsibility of car will fall on the owner.

Vedic Transporter Code #2
- A very comfortable car.
- Lots of shopping by the owner of this car.
- The car will be well decorated inside.
- Lots of music will be played in this car.
- Someone will always be transported in this car.

Vedic Transporter Code #3
- A party car that never miss a party.
- A very comfortable car that will be popular.
- Will experience problems with children in this car.
- A skinny person will drive this car a lot.
- Lots of books or papers in this car.
- A phone or TV system will be in this car.

Vedic Transporter Code #4
- A car that is solid and reliable
- This car can have body problems later.

Vedic Transporter Code #5
- You will drive this vehicle a great deal.
- Your car may be used for long distance travel.
- The owners of this car will enjoy romance and love.
- Air filters should be changed very often on this car.
- Problems with this car may involve the wheels, alignment or break repairs maybe required often.

Vedic Transporter Code #6
- Problems with this car may involve accidents, traffic tickets and collision.

- Make sure you have good insurance coverage and follow all rules.
- The body of this car may experience scratches or dents.
- Make sure you do regular tune-ups and maintenance as needed.
- Police will notice you very often while driving this car.
- You will have a high credit debt on or high payments.
- If you lease, it's better than buying outright.

Vedic Transporter Code #7

- A very quiet, comfortable and smooth driving with this car
- You will constantly be in deep thought while driving this car
- There may be religious pictures and air fresheners in this car
- A good car for you to take on a long drive.
- The only problems for this car will be the inside engine parts and the liquids such as the coolants, etc.

Vedic Transporter Code #8

- This car will be an expensive or luxury car fully loaded
- This car could be a limousine, town car or luxury sedan
- The price of this car will be high and the car will be attractive
- The owner will be someone who makes a lot of money or he or she could very well be in business
- This car will be expensive to maintain and will involve love affairs with the opposite sex
- This may be a sports car or a race car

Vedic Transporter Code #9

- Be careful of accidents and breakdowns while driving
- Avoid driving too much if this is an old car

- You will experience traffic tickets and court problems while owning this car
- The cooling system and pumps are weak and will give problems
- Be prepared to spend lots of money on repairs etc.
- You could experience an accident that totals the car
- Make sure you ask a priest to bless the car before driving.

Chapter 32

The Reincarnation Code

What Happens to the Soul After It Leaves the Body?

In twelve days' time, the angels of Death lead the soul to a different planet in the Universe, according to the karmic actions performed by the soul while it was on Earth. Depending on the kind of experience chosen for the next birth, the soul then enters the womb of a woman. First, a nucleus is formed in the umbilical region, which splits into bifurcated seed. The fetus is then evolved with frothy exudation. Blood and muscles are formed thereafter when the lump may weigh a milligram then it is said to sprout. Limbs begin to grow; fingers develop; eyes, nose, nails and so on become evident. Hair begins to grow on the body and the head; the child is placed in a topsy-turvy position and is born in the ninth month.

Then the most delusive Universe begins to envelop him as he proceeds from infancy to child. Then, he dies and reaps the fruit of his different activities of action caught in the cogs of the wheel of worldly existence.

It would be difficult to provide all the Vedic codes of Reincarnation in this book, however below I have listed some of the most important ones.

The Vedic Code of Science has a tremendous amount of knowledge about past, present and future lives. I hope we will be able provide this precious information in later publications.

Vedic Science Codes of Reincarnation

- A life coming back from hell becomes born of sinful who accepting gifts from a fallen man takes birth in a lower stratum.
- A beggar, on returning from hell, is born as a worm.
- A student defrauding his teacher is born as a dog.
- Mentally lusting after his teacher's wife he undoubtedly is born as a dog. *Alike dishonoring friends he is reborn as an ass.
- A person harassing the parents is reborn as a tortoise.
- If an employee trusted by his employer and partaking of his food deceives him out of delusion he is reborn as a monkey after death.
- One who misappropriate funds or trust of property is reborn a worm.
- A person who is always envious of others is born again a Demona.
- A man committing breach of trust is reborn a fish.
- A person hoarding barley grains is reborn a mouse after death.
- A person committing rape on other men's wives is reborn as a vile wolf.
- A person pursuing an affair with his brother's teacher or other elders is reborn as a pig.
- If a person causes any impediment to a sacrifice, act of charity or performance of a love connection he shall be reborn as a worm.
- If a person takes food without being thankful to god for it is reborn as a crow.
- A man insulting his elder brother is born again as a crane.
- A low class person ravishing a religious woman is born again as a worm.
- If he makes her pregnant as a result of his vile act he is reborn as a white ant eating away wood and trees.
- An ungrateful wretch is born successively as bacteria worm, locust and scorpion.

- A person abducting an unarmed person is reborn as a mule.
- A slayer of women and infants is reborn as a worm.
- A person stealing cooked food is born again as a fly.
- One who steals cooked rice is born a cat, sesame seeds a mouse, butter a mongoose and sheat-fish a crow.
- A man stealing honey is reborn as a gnat.
- A thief of fried pie is reborn an ant.
- The thief of (irrigation) water is reborn as a crow.
- A stealer of timber is born as a Harita bird or a pigeon.
- The stealer of a gold vessel is reborn as a worm.
- A stealer of cotton garments is born as a cane.
- A fire-thief becomes a stork.
- A thief of paints and vegetables is born a peacock.
- If a person steals any red object he is born as a cakora bird.
- If a man steals auspicious scents he is born as a mole.
- A thief of rabbits is reborn as a rabbit.
- A thief of peacock's plumes or a woman's girdle or any other ornament is reborn as a eunuch.
- A stealer of wooden pieces is born again as a grass worm.
- If a person steals flowers he is reborn a poor beggar.
- If a person steals lac-juice he is born again as a lame man.
- A thief of greens and vegetables is reborn as a Harita bird;
- A person stealing stored water is reborn as a Cataka bird.
- A person illegally occupying another man's house undergoes hardships as a disabled person in the next life.
- A person stealing grasses, hedges, creepers and barks of these is born again as a tree. This is the same in the case of the stealers of cow, gold, etc.

- A stealer of knowledge (a person who does not pay for instructions received) undergoes hardships as a dumb person.
- If a person casts butter and other offerings in evil places or fire he is reborn as a man suffering from chronic impairment of digestion.
- The characteristic features of those who would suffer a difficult after life would be those people who are involved in scandalizing others, ingratitude, outraging the limits of decency, ruthlessness, cruelty, attachment to other men's wives, stealing another man's property, blasphemy, harassing and deceiving others, and miserliness.

The characteristic features of those that have had a happy sojourn in heaven and are reborn are:
- Sympathetic towards all living beings, pleasant conversation,
- Believe in a supreme region, helping in return, truthfulness,
- Wholesome advice to others, belief in the authority of government
- Spiritually devoted to teachers. Angel, divine sages
- Enlightened sages, etc., association with good men,
- Eager to perform noble deeds and friendship.

The Vedic Reincarnation Code consists of three divisions of Vedic Science Codes that involve the past lives, the present life and the future lives. In this chapter, we are going to look only at the previous Life Code from the divisions of past lives. We may take a look also at the immediate future that will follow your present Life Codes.

In this discussion of your previous life we refer to this code as the Vedic Previous Life Code. Because of the enormity of the discussion on all of your many past lives, we are unable to put it in such a short chapter. However,

I hope that with a glimpse of your Previous Life Code you will be able to use this information to help you create a better present life and you will be more prepared to face your next reincarnation in a blessed way.

To know your Vedic Previous Life Code, Table 32.1 is used with your Vedic Birth Code as the key:

TABLE 32:1 -YOUR PREVIOUS LIFE CODES

VEDIC BIRTH CODE	VEDIC PREVIOUS LIFE CODE	VEDIC BIRTH CODE	VEDIC PREVIOUS LIFE CODE
1	9	6	5
2	1	7	6
3	2	8	7
4	3	9	8
5	4	1	9

Vedic Previous Life Code #1
- You are a person who held a position of dominance, ruling, leadership, and were in charge in many locations where you lived and worked.
- You craved love and affection and experienced loneliness.
- You did not understand cooperation and sympathy, which is why you are forced to recognize those in this life.
- You wanted to be heard but couldn't speak.
- You could have been abused and did not get your desires fulfilled.
- Because you did everything by yourself, you could not obtain all the material things you wanted, sometimes you starved for food and attention.
- People may have admired you as a leader, but it was lonely at the top.

Vedic Previous Life Code #2
- You were involved in a food business or restaurant.
- You were in a successful marriage relationship.
- You were selfish in romance so you did not want many children.
- You served many people at the expense of your own comfort.
- You owned lots of jewelry and dresses.
- You were either a singer, a musician or writer of music.

Vedic Previous Life Code #3
- You had many children and did a lot of babysitting.
- You had a very comfortable life and lived a long life.
- You worked very little and made lots of money.
- Your family considered you a little princess or prince.
- You were involved in acting and many social events.

Vedic Previous Life Code #4
- You may have been a farmer or you live in a farm.
- You worked very hard and craved to be free and to travel.
- You were suppressed from being free to say what you wanted.
- You felt imprisoned by your duties and your employment.
- You wanted to do your own business but couldn't do it.
- You were underpaid and over worked.
- You may have worked in factory, manufacturing industry or a gardener.

Vedic Previous Life Code #5
- You were a traveler and did not have time to spend with family so in this life you are forced to deal with family responsibilities.

- Because of your fate of being controlled by others, you are afraid of losing control in this life.
- You were involved in politics, positions of power or conspired against others in power, so in this life you seek positions of power and may become powerful in politics.
- You had many lovers in your last life and as a result because you deceived many, you may have love problems in this life.
- Because of your intense love for pleasure and relaxation in the last life, you will be stuck with lots of responsibilities in this life.
- You may have been involved in sales, airline industries, transportation or robbery.

Vedic Previous Life Code #6
- You could have been a king, queen, president or political leader of a country.
- You may have abused many people in your past life either as a princess or prince of a castle and therefore you could become an alcoholic in this life.
- You were involved in legal proceedings or may have been a lawyer.
- You could have been a criminal or a police officer or court leader.
- You may have been a soldier in the military or a warrior of the king.
- You were a very responsible person and took good care of the family or the community.
- You could have been the victim of jealousy and anger.

Vedic Previous Life Code #7
- You were a religious leader or priest in a temple or a great devotee of the lord.
- You may been a great religious singer or musician in your last life.

- You had all the blessings of God but yearned for the wealth of the rich.
- You were an alcoholic, drug addict or medical doctor.
- You were involved in hospitals, temples, monasteries and churches.
- You may have been born in India, Italy or in a holy land.
- You had great difficulty in marriage in your last life.
- Because of that you will be married to a rich partner or actor.

Vedic Previous Life Code #8

- You were very rich & wealthy, and may have been a queen or king.
- You were so involved in enjoying luxury that in this life you have been denied that pleasure.
- If you were a spendthrift in the last life and wasted wealth then in this life you have very little money and you will struggle a great deal.
- You were involved in movies, investments, and the stock market, so in this life you will lose a great deal in your investments.
- You were involved in having many partners and lovers and so in this life you will have difficulty with love life.

Vedic Previous Life Code #9

- You struggled a great deal and worked like a slave in the last life.
- You had very little freedom and were dominated by your peers.
- You were not allowed to lead you life without interference.
- You participated in bad worship and illegal activities and could have been incarcerated.

- You suffered from major illnesses and diseases and may have been in the hospital or experienced sudden death.
- You could have been a very famous or very notorious personality.
- You may have dreams in this life of having been on ships at sea.
- You could have been a prison officer or judge or political leader.
- You may have been a great priest or highly respected and intelligent guru or religious leader.

Chapter 33

The Karmic Code – Results of Hate and Love

There is an order in the Universe in which we live and each of our actions has a profound effect on that order. The Universe moves to correct itself depending upon the action performed. When we hate, for instance, God devises a way to teach us love. This concept is akin to the scientific law of equilibrium. When a system, which was functioning in an orderly manner, is thrown into chaos by some action or force, the system quickly reacts to restore that order and reverts back from a state of disequilibrium to its original state of equilibrium.

Ever notice that Hindus, who hate Muslims, usually end up with a Muslim son- or daughter-in-law? The same is true for Muslims who hate Hindus or whites who hates blacks. Observational experience has shown that families will end up with other families with whom hatred exists between parents or members of those families. History has shown that British people, who hate people of other nations, usually end up with grandsons and granddaughters from those very nations. Take for example the hatred by Muslims of the Americans, they created the karma for Ann Halabi making her Queen Noor of Jordan and Americans becoming the friends of Israel.

The impact of slavery had a profound effect on what social scientists today refer to as the "browning of America." Whites who hated Africans, eventually making them slaves, ended up having to share their sons, daughters and country with the very blacks that they hated. Hatred is the key word. The Universe reacts to hatred and returns the Karma accordingly.

God orchestrates your life situation and places you in a position to face that hate so that you will be able to understand it and enable yourself to deal with it in a positive way. All religions teach love. When you love, you are acting in concert with the Universe and you will not have to go through the hard learning process to convert your hate into love. You do not have to suffer because of your dislike for things or people.

If Hindus love and accept Muslims or Christians, then there will no need for God to teach them and so this unquestionable acceptance automatically relieves you of the karma. This is why Hinduism is a non-violent religion; it encompasses all people as parts of God. If Muslims, who hate other people because of religion, try to love and understand them, then the Muslims will not have to worry later about dealing with that result of one of their children falling in love and marrying into that other family.

If the daughter, who hates her alcoholic father, tries to understand why he is a drunkard and extends her love to him, then she will not have to be forced to accept a husband, who will turn out to be a drunkard later in order to teach her acceptance. As you can see, this Love-Hate Karma affects each and every one of us in all aspects of life. Finding happiness is so easy. All you have to do is love and accept everyone in your life, and automatically, you will not have to go through the negative consequences and be tested on that particular quality of life.

Karma, in a way, is like heredity. If your parents hated something or some person, you will hate that thing or person as well. For example, when there are feuds between two families, the children of each would fall in love with each other, and then the parents are placed in a position to decide according to their own karma.

In my own experience as a swami, I have noticed that when a person creates conflict with their boss and leaves

214

a job, later they have a hard time finding a good job, until he comes to some resolve with that lesson that haunts him from that previous employment.

Karma – How It Is Created and Fulfilled

In love connections, if the daughter treats her father badly, she ends up with a bad husband, if the son treats his mother bad, then he ends up with a bad wife. In some cases, if a woman aborts a child that she wanted at the time of conception, the next child would be a disabled or problem child that will affect all members of the family. Since father and mother are the creators of the child, whatever hurt the father or mother experiences from the child, then the child must experience in his or her own life.

> The Universe is very exact. The rule of the Universe is - Take any action you wish to perform, but be warned!
> Do not hurt anyone in the process or else you will have to pay for it with your own experiences.

Unless the experience is fulfilled, you cannot move on with your life. However, if proper remedies are taken and your previous bad actions are spiritually removed then you may be able to cut short the negative experiences and follow the next level in your life in a positive manner.

However each time you decide to make a change in your life again, you must make that change at an appropriate time, day, month, year, cycle and so on. *A change must take place only when the time is ready.*

To know when that moment is appropriate you must see a swami or a Hindu Vedic Science consultant. That is why we must have a guru or a teacher, who will guide you with knowledge and advice, which is the key to correcting your past karma and experiences.

That is the reason for the Vedic Science of Karma. This science sometimes is related to a science called

Jyotish, which is based on the law of reincarnation. The fact that this present life span is not unique, but part of a long cycle of experience which stretches far back into the past and even today, prepares itself for the future. Numerous times are we born into a new physical body, and we experience the joys.

We are not on this journey alone. According to those teachers, who possess knowledge of spiritual law, we journey in groups. We reincarnate with those we have loved, those we have hated, those who have helped us, those with whom we have suffered. We may find ourselves in different or even alternating relationships - at times as master or as servant, at times as parent or as child or as husband, or wife and so on.

Karma – How It Is Created and Fulfilled

All of these experiences help us to understand precisely how another individual feels in any situation, to feel with him until slowly we learn in detail how to treat another as we would like to be treated in the same circumstances. To a considerable extent, these lessons are in accord with the law of cause and effect, in the west known as Newton's Law of Action vs. Reaction, known in the Eastern religions as karma and in   Christianity as "what you sow you shall reap". This universal law works in parallel with that of reincarnation and ensures that we are born into the correct situations and with the proper group of individuals to balance our debts for past errors and wrong doing – or as a reward for "good acts".

The soul is presented with a full picture of its numerous incarnations on Earth. Gradually it begins to grasp a vision of those gifts of the spirit which, when developed to perfection, will enable it to make its own contribution to the joy and peace of the whole. It realizes that only further learning experiences in a physical body will develop these gifts; thus it senses the need between reincarnations.

The doctrine of karma, though originating on the East, has become increasingly better known and appreciated by the Western world during the past several decades. Everything in the Universe is brought under the influence of karma, the law of cause and effect. Nothing escapes it. Through the study of the Karmic Codes, as given by the Vedic Code of Science, we can gain a better understanding of karma and the kind of experiences one can expect during our lifetime – and, more importantly, how mistakes or previous lives can be corrected.

Just knowing your Vedic Birth Code can identify the tests you have to go through in this life. Awareness of a problem is already a 50% of the cure. Knowing the problems you have to face will help you to cure them faster. Below you can find out about your Karma by obtaining your Vedic Birth Code from Chapter 6 and reading the information under that Birth Code.

Vedic Birth Code #1 – Your Karmic Tests in This Life
Independence, dominating, originality, constantly occupied, leadership, career opportunities, business opportunities, knowledge, single, alone, loneliness, solitary confinement, hot, self, body, head, can be destroyed by too much independence and domination. Conflicts with 5, 8, 7, and 4. Attainment, drive, success, ambition, intention, mentality, god force, seek praise, impatient, boastful, conceited, large scale projects.

Vedic Birth Code #2 – Your Karmic Tests in This Life
Love connection, romance, true love, affection, kindness, generous, loved by the people, popularity, partnership, spouse, woman, emotion, cooperation, love for the world, self sacrificing, dedicated love connection partner, can be destroyed by divorce. Conflicts with 7, 8, 4, 1 and 2. Seek association, crave love, understanding, like comforts, not ambitious, doubt, force between love and hate, subordinate, sensitive, give lot of love and affection.

Vedic Birth Code #3 – Your Karmic Tests in This Life
Expression of oneself, spiritual speeches, throat, mouth, tongue, youth, children, pregnancy, birth, sastras, reading, immaturity, communication, telephone, telegraph, educational courses, school, teacher, bargain shopping, publishing, sickness of children, losses for non-religious individuals, pleasant, childish, egotistical, will not admit defeat, make decisions without thinking, untidy, can be destroyed by abortion (women) and fickleness (men). Conflicts with 3, 6, 7 and 1. Triangle, bountiful harvest, good luck, fruitfulness, steam, good fortune, acquisition, works well with 2, 4, 8 and 5, friendly, outgoing, seek happiness, beauty in all people.

Vedic Birth Code #4 – Your Karmic Tests in This Life
Work, career, hard work, industry, manufacturing, stress, tension, rheumatism, pain, overtime, low pay, real estate, rental, inheritance, antiques, lawyers, difficulties obtaining a job, lover of antiques, repairs to home or cars, can be destroyed by laziness and landlord tenant relationships. Conflicts with 2, 5, 6 and 1. Down to Earth, simple, body of man, struggle, manifestation, order, growth, endurance, accomplishment, discovery, boundaries, sacrifice through work, drudgery, limitation, lover of tradition, dependable, security, stability, lack of money.

Vedic Birth Code #5 – Your Karmic Tests in This Life
Sex, romance, illicit affairs, falsehood, others people's money, deceit, travel abroad, long distance travel, sudden changes, vacation, false allegations, long distance calls, beauty, sexual bliss, concerns with body only not the mind, sex after first meeting, movement from one home to the next, dedicated love connection partner, great sense of humor, good story teller, science fiction writer, can be destroyed by illicit sexual affairs and gossip. Conflicts with 1, 4, 5, and 9. Possible evil, activity, expansion, freedom, independence, anxiety, worry, restlessness,

commerce and travel, short, magnetic, follow easy road in life, above average intelligence, deceiver.

Vedic Birth Code #6 – Your Karmic Tests in This Life
Man, jealousy, love connection, divorce, quarrels, misunderstanding, ego, enmity, quarrel with relatives, responsibility, court, government, sickness, prolonged diseases, possible domestic happiness, money through spouse, power, political, repairs to home, accidents, repairs to cars, election, group meetings, purchase of new home, selfishness, government/court problems, enemies, quarrel with co-workers, egotistical, likes to be in charge, high temper, military oriented, pain in lower back, high blood pressure, can be destroyed by anger and meat eating. Conflicts with 3, 4, 9 and 1. Loneliness, secure love connection, conflict by passion, antagonism, justice, obligations.

Vedic Birth Code #7 – Your Karmic Tests in This Life
Criticism, fault finding, religion, spirituality, meetings with holy people, visitation to the temple, low income, few opportunities, secret meetings and secret thoughts, self consciousness, self inspection, looking for perfection which does not exist, reserved, complaining over petty things, wants to be right always, news of death far away, association with elders, priests, and people in authority, sleepiness, slow movement, mental tiredness, unable to think outwardly, hidden feelings, spiritual teacher, guru, temples, comfortable homes, delay in business and profits, criminals, astrology, does not like to be criticized, menstrual periods, will perform religious actions, can be destroyed by ego and criticism, drugs and addiction, poisonous tongue. Conflicts with 8, 9, 6, and 2. Spirit of God, royalty, honor, fame, wisdom, philosophical, loves to be conservative, lives in the clouds, likes to daydream, revolutionary in ideas, prefers to live alone, thinks he is better than others.

Vedic Birth Code #8 – Your Karmic Tests in This Life
Karmic debts, money, finance, property, investments, assets, success in career, promotion, raises, honor, gain from government, profitable business, fame, financial problems, gain from relationships, pleasure with lovers, luxury, extravagance, expensive shopping, cheerfulness, steadiness, victory over enemies, receiving money lent, business, can be destroyed by inability to control money and waste of material possessions. Conflicts with 7, 2, 1 and 9. Scale of justice, lover of big business, seeker of power, gives out confidence and courage.

Vedic Birth Code #9 – Your Karmic Tests in This Life
Fame, accident, government, IRS, law, philosophy, dealing with officials of the law, loss of money, sickness, pain, incurable disease, strangers, illness to children, pilgrimage, spiritual advancement, burial place, cemetery, separation, imprisonment, legal difficulties, civil court, criminal court, prophetic dreams, spiritual publishing, tension, domestic unhappiness, death, difficult travels, break in education, death of older person, quarrel with co-workers, possible pregnancy, astrologers, death from incurable diseases, will perform religious ceremonies, end of all things, accusation of murder, fraud or rape, etc., curse of Brahmins or religious individuals, can be destroyed by self denial, alcohol and God. May conflict with all. Seeker of knowledge, self sacrificing, want to help the world, energy, penetration, regeneration, privacy, violence, impulsive, end of things, fruits of harvest, imperfection, grief, story of job, zeal, failure, disciple, bad nerves. Conflicts with #9, #6 and #7. Learn to recognize now that your past is as changeable as your future. You may choose to realize aspects of your past life long since forgotten, and now put them to positive, constructive, and healthy use. This is what is called free will.

The past will create the future...the present will correct both past errors and future outcomes.

Chapter 34

The Meditation Code

The Vedic Code of Science views meditation as a science of mind over matter. The mind processes energy in the form of thoughts and creation. Its creative energy has the ability to create changes in the spiritual world. Because of the constant amount of energy used in the mind to control the body every so often our energy gets dissipated or highly negative. The negative energy of the mind can create health problems, which can cause malfunction of our physical body.

Have you ever noticed that when you meet certain people, they seem to have a calming effect on your mind while if you encounter certain others, the effect is very negative? Well, this is because of the energy field that is contained in the human body of one-person conflicts or merges positively with the energy field of the other person. As we go through our daily lives we come into contact with all kinds of energy levels or energy blocks. The food we eat, the clothes we wear, they way we sleep, the location energy of the places we visit all contribute towards our human energy aura. Whenever this energy aura around the human body is disturbed or irritated in a state of non-equilibrium, we experience low energy or the need to sleep longer. We also experience things like the inability to control our emotions, which may lead to anger, frustration and conflicts with others.

To repair auric energy around the body, the Vedic Code of Science recommends following the Vedic Meditation Code, which calms and repairs the broken parts of auric energy around the body. Each person has their own individual response to meditative energy and methods. The main cause of a person's problem with meditation is that most people think that they are able to control the

Universe. Thus, they give up their faith in the fact that the Universe is more powerful than they are and do not recognize that the Universe is the higher power.

The first thing we should realize before commencing meditation is to accept the fact that the Universe is always alive and moving as energy around us. We must realize that we cannot change the movements of the Sun or the Moon or the planets or the wind or we cannot control the tides of the ocean. They control us; we have to conform to their rules. We must learn to bow and give up our ego with the thought that we think that we are in control but we are not. We must learn to bow gracefully to the Universe and realize also that we are but a speck in the solar system of the Universe.

In the following paragraphs, I have described the nine methods of Vedic meditation procedures that will help you to meditate in the appropriate way so that you can achieve the ultimate relaxation level in your life. Only one of the nine methods applies to your life according to your Vedic Birth Code. The recommended techniques will help you achieve a maximum amount of positive energy from your prayers, meditation or yoga sessions.

In the following paragraphs, use your Vedic Birth Code from Chapter 6 to get an idea as to how you should go about doing your meditation and controlling your own energy. The following paragraphs describe and recommend some meditation methods and techniques that you can use to guide yourself into proper meditation.

Meditation Techniques for Vedic Birth Code #1

- Your primary focus is on leadership and prestige.
- It is recommended that you meditate for a maximum of fifteen minutes. If you go any further than 15 minutes there may be difficulties with your mental concentration. To ensure concentration, be sure that you are alone and that you slow the racing of your mind. When meditating, try to think of all of the

things that worry you and then try to find solutions to these worries.
- A quiet room in a building or a high platform is suitable for your meditation

Meditation Techniques for Vedic Birth Code #2
- Your primary mediation focus is on love, love connection and serving others.
- Learn to meditate on your spending and your desire for material things.
- Use your meditation moments for building your inner strength so that people cannot take advantage of your kindness.
- Learn to meditate on the people who return your love for them; do not try to buy anybody's love.
- All your prayers should be toward appreciating the simple things that people do for you.
- Do your meditation in a congregation or in a shrine or in front of an altar.

Meditation Techniques for Vedic Birth Code #3
- Your primary meditation focus is children, expression and social relationship.
- You should meditate and put light around your children instead of worrying about them all the time; your light protects them.
- You should meditate on changing your childish ways and think of those thoughts that make you mature in your thinking.
- In your meditation avoid ways of thinking how you can control others; instead see how much they love you.
- Remembering and replaying childhood fantasies makes you feel good in meditation.
- A nursery, in front of a television video for meditation or a school is good for your meditation location.

Meditation Techniques for Vedic Birth Code #4

- Your primary meditation focus should be on your career and home.
- Learn to relax in your meditation as you are always stressed at your workplace.
- You should learn to schedule yourself for daily meditation for at least 15 minutes; it will help your energy for love.
- When meditating try to cool off the anger you acquire during the daily schedule and learn to forgive.
- Underground caves and rocks on the ground are good places for your meditation.

Meditation Techniques for Vedic Birth Code #5

- Your primary meditation focus is change and sexuality.
- Remember that God is watching you at all times, so learn to obey the rules of the Universe.
- You must meditate carefully before you venture on any illegal acts, as karma surely returns the lash.
- Meditate on business ideas, strategies and inventions, as this will help you become wealthier.
- Choose an ocean or natural location for your meditation, as the energy will be better there.

Meditation Techniques for Vedic Birth Code #6

- Your primary meditation focus is responsibility, frustration and family.
- You must realize that you are not in control of the Universe; God is.
- It's very hard for you to meditate, because you do not like to give up control very easily.
- You may be too protective of your family so you must give this job to God and let Him do it for you in your meditation.

- You get frustrated very easily so you need to meditate to calm yourself down when you think you are losing control.
- A military base, government house or a temple are good locations for your meditation

Meditation Techniques for Vedic Birth Code #7
- Your primary meditation focus is love and godly things.
- It is recommended that you meditate for at least 30 minutes, so as to slow your thoughts. While meditating you should always be in the lotus position of sitting with folded feet, with your thumb and forefinger touching. Your eyes should always be closed during meditation, as you are always looking at your inner self.
- A holy location, temple, mountain or place of worship is your best place for meditation.

Meditation Techniques for Vedic Birth Code #8
- Your primary meditation focus is wealth and luxury.
- It will be very difficult to meditate with your eyes closed; therefore it is recommended that you keep your eyes open during meditation. You meditate best when you have an object in front of you, such as a crystal ball or a candle.
- You must focus on the fact that money is not the source of happiness but inner peace is the greatest wealth.
- The more you meditate and pray so also your material desires are fulfilled.
- A monument, richly decorated room or building or office or work location is the best place for your meditation.

Meditation Techniques for Vedic Birth Code #9

- Your primary meditation focus should be on the struggle for progress, decision-making and health.
- Because of your confused state of mind, sometimes, you need to perform long meditation. Generally, half an hour to an hour is recommended. During this time, you are advised to calm your mind by having no doubts about the existence of God.
- Because of your changing beliefs, sometimes you accept the Universe and sometimes you don't. In your meditation session, learn to accept those things that you cannot change and change the things that only you have control over.

Meditation is recommend for you at least twice a day, because you have the ability to absorb negative energy very easily.

- Your meditation area should consist of incense burning and a fountain or waterfall next to you. The best place for your meditation is on the beach or at the seashore.
- Meditation, yoga and prayers are important for you to remove health problems, doubts and denials.
- Next a river, on the beach, close to reservoir or in a processing plant, under a tree or in a lonely place are all good locations.

Chapter 35

Destruction of the World Trade Center
As Explained by
The Vedic Code of Science

If we were to apply the Vedic Code of Science to the World Trade Center incident, we would observe some interesting correlation between what happened on 9/11 and certain events as well as with all the people that were involved. The Vedic Code of Science will attempt to provide a codified view as well as a logical explanation of why the Universe was presenting such an enigma that created such a storm of emotional change throughout the human world.

Let us take a look at the date itself – 9/11, which forms the Vedic Code 2, which, as indicated in our Table in Chapter 7, is a code of "human relationship."

The day was the 11th day of September.

The flight number of the 1st plane that hit was 11.

The number of people onboard that plane was 92 (9+2=11).

The Twin Towers had 110 floors (1+1+0=11).

The Twin Towers standing side by side look like the number 11.

The number of days from January 1st to 9/11 was 254 (2+5+4=11).

New York State is the 11th state of the union.

July 4th as the Vedic Birth Code of the United States is 11 (7+4=11).

Looking at the names involved in this event will indicate some interesting connections to the number 11.

New York City - 11 letters

Afghanistan - 11 letters

George W. Bush - 11 letters
Osama bin Laden - 11 letters
Mohamed Atta - 1st hijacker to hit WTC - 11 letters
Aran Alshehi - 2nd hijacker to hit WTC - 11 letters
Rudy Guliani - Mayor of New York City - 11 letters
Ramzi Yousef - person who unsuccessfully bombed
    WTC in 1993 - 11 letters
Colin Powell - US Secretary of State - 11 letters
USA Pentagon - 11 letters
Keith Miller - NBC newsman stationed in Islamabad
    - 11 letters
Daniel Pearl - reporter killed in Pakistan - 11 letters

After all of the above, one might ask what does #11 have to do with destruction of the WTC? Well, if we were to apply Vedic mathematics to the #11 (1+1) and reduce it to the result of 2, the Vedic Code of love and relationships, we can conclude the following:

Adding the number 2 to the Birth Code of the president of the United States, George W. Bush, you get 6 (2+4=6), the Vedic Code that reflects war, destruction and power struggle. Again, if we apply the number 2 from the number 11 to the year 2002, the year following destruction of the WTC, we get the number 6 (2+2+0+0+2=6), the Vedic Code of War, destruction and power struggle (USA v UN on Iraq War). The US did go to war with Iraq.

We all know that the Book of Revelations in the Bible considers the number 666 an evil number. Please note that when we add the number 666 in Vedic mathematics (6+6+6), the result is 18, which is then further reduced to 9, the Vedic Code of death and termination. Well, if we were to take all the 11 numbers from the previous results and add each 11 to the year 2002, the result would be 66666666...for all the names and codes involve on the date of 9/11.

Applying the Vedic Code of death and termination – 9 – to the World Trade Center events, we find some interesting connections between this code and the people and dates involved.

If we take the Code of change (#5) and add it to the Birth Code of President Bush (#4), the result is Vedic Code 9; again death, destruction and power struggle related to the United States.

It was exactly 9 years before – in 1993 – when the first attempt was made to destroy the World Trade Center. If we take the Birth Code of the USA (2) and add it to the year 1993 (4), we get 6, which is the Vedic Code of struggle and war.

If we were to add the Vedic Code of War (6) to the year 2001 (3), the result is Vedic Code 9, the code of death and destruction (6+1001=8).

According to Vedic Science, the Eastern year for harvest begins every September of the Western year. According to Eastern timing, 2002 would be considered the year ruling at the time of the 9/11 events. If we were to take Western year 2001 and add it to the Eastern year of 2002 and then add it to the Event Code of 11, the result would be Vedic Code 9, the code of death and destruction.

If we take the Vedic Code of Travel (5) and add it to the year 2002, the result would be 9 (5+2002), the Vedic Code of death and destruction. We all know that the travel industry almost came to a halt and the airline and ground transportation industries for travelers suffered great losses. Traveling became very difficult and uncomfortable for a great many people in the United States and abroad. Many airlines filed bankruptcy in the courts and many people lost their money in the industry.

The New Millennium

There was a clear misconception by the world about the actual time when the new millennium started. The new millennium actually began on January 1, 2001; however, the whole world was led to believe that it started in January 2000 by the computer companies that installed the fear of Y2K disasters in the minds of people. Because of this, people did not realize that the world actually experienced a great renewal and awakening in the 9th month of the new millennium, really 2001.

A look at the years from 1989 (9) to the year 2001 (3) reveals an astounding continuity in the events that preceded 9/11/2001. Please bear in mind that if we were to take all the years from 600 BC to 1989, only the years 1899 and 1989 would add up to 27 or triple 9 (9+9+9). The world experienced significant changes in these years. Let us take a serious look at the years previous to the new millennium...the eventful 90s.

1989 - Communism took a fall and most of the countries in the world became democratic.

1990 - Violence increased considerably among the Middle Eastern countries starting with the letter "I" – Iran, Iraq, Israel. Saddam Hussein began to be troublesome to the USA.

1991 - The Gulf War between the US and Iraq took place, but was not effective enough to stop the power of Saddam Hussein. The war lasted 45 days, the time it takes for the planet Mars to traverse 30 degrees of the zodiac.

1992 - Osama bin Laden appeared as the Turban Terrorist, and the strongest hurricane ever to hit the US – Hurricane Andrew – caused enormous damage to the state of Florida.

1993 - Attempts to bomb and destroy the World Trade Center failed and the terrorist, Ramzi Yousef, swore that his organization would be back to destroy it, as he was being taken to prison.

1994 - The most renowned murder trial of the decade began – the O. J. Simpson case. The Eiffel Tower in Paris, France was the target of terrorists.

1995 - Over 200 US soldiers were killed in a US training center bombed by terrorists.

1996 - The apartment complex for Americans in Teheran, Iran was bombed by terrorists; many were killed.

1997 - Many tourists, including Americans, were killed in a bombing incident in Egypt, again by terrorists.

1998 - The US Embassy in Africa was destroyed by a terrorist bombing.

1999 - The US sailor ship was destroyed at sea by terrorism. The largest sex scandal trial ever, that of US President Bill Clinton, began.

2000 - The election scandal of the US – the people had a choice – election or selection of the US president. George Bush won by Supreme Court decision, the first time in the history of the USA.

2001 - The destruction of the World Trade Center occurred exactly 9 years after the first attempt in 1993. The world experienced a new awakening towards the religion of Islam.

2002 - Another member of the Bush family – George W. – launched a pre-emptive war against Saddam Hussein of Iraq, a promise kept by the Elder Bush that he would return to get Saddam. The planet Mars comes closest to the Earth in centuries.

Nostradamus predicted centuries before the rise of the Turban Warrior from the East that we saw played out here in history. The vents of the "destructive 90s" led eventually to the rude awakening of human existence after the destruction of the World Trade Center in 2001.

As you can see, the Vedic Code of Science clearly indicates that death and destruction were events that Nostradamus predicted, that in the 9th month of the new millennium, the "New City" would face destruction as it was struck by two "birds from above. The 90s were a period pre-empting this reawakening of the human race. Because of all the world events that took place in the previous century, which are considered negative, the Earth and the Universe has created a reaction that will help bring about a great change in human thinking and awareness. All religions will be questioned about their validity in being genuine in the progress of human thought. People will question whether astrology, spirituality and other forms of worship are really helping them in their lives. People will seek other forms of explanations for life and the future of the world. People will seek more technical details on how to be safer in the world and enjoy their family lives in a more secure way.

Only in times of distress or war that mankind seeks other means or methods of making or preserving peace on Earth. Only in times of suffering will people seek to come closer to God. To illustrate my point, let us look at the following story, called "Light vs. Darkness".

At one time in the Universe, there was an argument between LIGHT and DARKNESS. LIGHT insisted that she was more important to humans because she provided enlightenment, comfort, wealth, and beauty to them. DARKNESS disagreed, saying he was more important to humans because whenever he provided humans with arrogance, discomfort, poverty, and suffering, they would seek Godly messages and the advice of holy people. Since both LIGHT and DARKNES could not come to an agreement as to which one was more important, they sought the advice of the CREATOR. Feeling he would appear biased if he made a choice, the CREATOR decided to send them to the UNIVERSE. On their arrival there, the UNIVERSE welcomed both LIGHT and DARKNES and smiled, saying, "You are both important, LIGHT and DARKNESS. However, LIGHT, you are important only when you are coming into a person's life...and DARKNESS, you are very important only when you are leaving a person's life."

As you can see from the story above, humans, the Universe, and the Earth must be so balanced that light and darkness cannot affect them unevenly. People need to learn to enjoy the world in equilibrium before they can live happily.

Chapter 36

Special Note on the Power of Vedic Code #6 – The Vedic Science Code of Kali

Small droplets of water condensing into storm clouds and falling earthward through cold layers of the atmosphere cannot "think." Yet one of these droplets, when it freezes, forms a flat hexagonal crystal. Countless billions of them comprise tiny snowflakes, each with six sides or arms – and each one different than all the others. No two ever alike, infinite variation and endless beauty. How does this happen? Why don't they sometimes have eight or ten sides or four?

A snowflake is a crystal of frozen water; a diamond is a crystal of "frozen" carbon. One is formed in the atmosphere, the other within the mantle of the Earth. One has six sides, the other 12. Each seems to conform to the geomagnetic field and/or celestial magnetic field. They cannot "think." They have no instinct, let alone reason; therefore, exogenous forces must act upon them.

Distant stars, great nations and tiny snowflakes all are inextricably intertwined. Weather conditions are strongly responsive to the crystallizing 60-degree angle between planets. This 60-degree (hexagon) was considered by all ancient civilizations to be "sacred." Two perfect triangles of 120 degrees when placed together form the symbol of Judaism, the Star of David. Each point of this star is 60 degrees to the next.

Bees all over the world build hexagonal honeycombs. It is "unthinkable" that bees, of their own intelligence, consciously agree to this standard. Only recently have engineers discovered that the hexagon is the strongest, most economical storage bin imaginable. Yet bees have always "known" this, but how? By instinct? If so, exactly what is this instinct? How does it differ from free choice?

How do bees all over the world (ever since bees were "invented") build six-sided storage bins for their honey? They've always done it and probably will continue doing so for as long as there are bees.

In the Vedic Code of Science, 6 is considered a code that represents power, destruction, frustration and great emotional upheaval in relationships between all things. The Vedic Code of 6 represents the influences of war, conflicts between people, war between countries, separation of couples and such things as mortgages, debts, credit cards and loans. You'll find that the police or security forces of a country are represented by the Vedic Code #6. An analysis of the Birth Codes of all the police or military members would reveal a predominant number of them that add up to the Vedic Code of 6.

In the Vedic Code of Science, the God of negative time and destruction of evil is known as Kali, the sixth form of the female goddesses. She is known as the caretaker of the rules of the Universe. When the rules are broken and evil thoughts, acts or intentions threaten the Universe, Kali is the one who corrects the person or destroys the evil permanently.

People with Birth Codes that add up to the Vedic Code 6 usually experience a lot of traffic tickets in their life, court problems and accidents, if they live a negative lifestyle. If they live a positive lifestyle, they will experience power, luxury, great reputation in their career, family inheritance and popularity. Usually getting a government position helps to uplift the life of Kali people in a positive manner.

The year 1961 is made up of the numbers 6 and 9. When turned upside down, the numbers remain the same.

The number 9 has remarkable inversion properties. When reversed, it becomes a 6. When added to 6 it becomes 15, which if you add 1+5, you get 6. If we take the number 133335 and add up the digits, the result is 9. If we take the reverse of this number 533331 and add them to the original number, the result is 666,666, a double form of evil.

The 6th planet from the Sun is Saturn. The number 6 also rules Mars. Both of these planets are considered negative planets in astrological science.

The Vedic Code of 6 rules such things as violence, assassinations, violent deaths and separations. Interestingly, the highest office with the most power is the office of American president. The first president, George Washington, had a Birth Code of 6 (February 22). President Harrison, whose Birth Code was 2 (February 9), when added to April 4, 1841, you get the Day Code of 6, when he died in office.

President Abraham Lincoln, whose Birth Code was 5 (February 12), was assassinated and died in office. The day he died, Vedic Code 1 (April 15), when added to his Birth Code, gives the Vedic Code of 6, which indicates violent death. President William McKinley, who had a Birth Code of 3 (January 29), when added to the day he was shot in office (September 6), gives the Death Code of 9. McKinley died 8 days later on September 14, 1901.

President Warren Harding, whose Birth Code was 4 (November 2), when added to the Day Code (August 2) gives the Vedic Code of 6. He died in office after a heart attack. The Vedic Code of 6 (November 22) was also ruling at the time that President Kennedy was shot.

The first President Bush, elected in 1989, has a Birth Code of 9 (June 12). He was the first US president to take America into war after Viet Nam. If you remember also that President Lyndon Johnson, the 36th (Vedic Code 9) US president, whose Birth Code was 8 (August 27), elected in a year (1963), which when added to his Birth

Code results in 9 (code of struggle). He was the president that started the Viet Nam War.

Bill Clinton, whose Birth Code is 9, was troubled by terrorist bombings throughout his term in office. He was also the first president to be impeached by the House of Representatives.

The present President, George W. Bush, whose Birth Code is 4 (July 6), when added to the birthday of America (July 4) comes out to the Vedic Code of 6, the code of war. He restarted his father's legacy of war in Iraq. Please note his inaugural Day Code 2 (January 20), when added to his Birth Code, results in the Vedic Code 6. Hence, as long as he is president of the United States, the country will be at war.

It will take a strong personality like Hillary Clinton to take us out of war. Please note that the planet Mars, which started its journey toward Earth when George W. Bush took office, is going to recede after the 2006 elections, hence the return of the troops.

Appendix 1

The Other Vedic Codes

YOUR WORLD CODE
THE COUNTRY CODE
THE STREET CODE
THE TELEPHONE CODE
THE BUSINESS PARTNERSHIP CODE
THE ENEMY CODE
THE SEQUENCE CODE
THE DIET CODE
THE LONGEVITY CODE
THE SATURN EFFECT CODE
THE HATE CODE
THE STAGES OF LIFE CODE
THE DEATH CODE
THE INSANITY CODE
THE ORAL SEX CODE
THE ANCESTRAL CODE
THE LAST CHILD CODE
THE HOUR CODE
THE VEDIC CODE OF BRAMHA
THE VEDIC CODE OF DURGA
THE VEDIC CODE OF VISHNU
THE VEDIC CODE OF RUDRA
THE VEDIC CODE OF NARAYAN
THE VEDIC CODE OF KALI
THE VEDIC CODE OF SHIVA
THE VEDIC CODE OF LAXMI
THE VEDIC CODE OF INDRA
THE VEDIC CODE OF YAMA
THE UNIVERSAL CODE
THE YEARLY CODES

Appendix 2

Famous People & Their Vedic Birth Codes

"Some are born great, some achieve greatness, and some have greatness thrust upon them." – William Shakespeare

You may use the information in this chapter to test the Science of Vedic Codes. Using the codes provided, you can observe the characteristics and personality of famous people and see if they match your Vedic Code analysis.

Name	Birthdate	Vedic Birth Code#
Lord Russell	August 12	1
Empress Eugene	May 5, 2006	1
Mesmer	May 23	1
Karl Marx	May 5	1
Fahrenheit	May 14	1
Oliver Cromwell	April 24	1
Sir Isaac Newton	December 25	1
Bloody Queen Mary	February 17	1
Theodore Roosevelt	October 27	1
General Gordon	January 28	2
Annie Besant	October 1	2
Captain Cook	October 28	2
Nathaniel Hawthorne	July 4	2
Duke of Windsor	June 23	2
Duke of Marlborough	May 24	2
Mary, Queen of Scots	December 8	2
Queen Victoria	May 24	2
William Wordsworth	April 7	2
Rousseau	April 16	2

Name	Birthdate	Vedic Birth Code#
King Edward VII	November 9	2
William Garfield	November 19	3
Mahatma Gandhi	October 2	3
Lal Bahadur Shastri	October 2	3
Swedenborg	January 29	3
Thomas Hood	May 23	3
Queen Josephine	June 23	3
Robert Browning	May 7	3
Kepler	December 27	3
Woodrow Wilson	December 28	4
Queen Alexandra	December 1	4
Thomas Edison	February 11	4
Marie Antoinette	November 2	4
Thomas Chatterton	November 20	4
Ramsay MacDonald	October 12	4
Louis XVI	August 23	4
Cecil Rhodes	July 6	4
Ralph Waldo Emerson	June 25	4
Leopold II of Belgium	April 9	4
Ulysses S. Grant	April 27	4
Louis Kossuth	April 27	4
James Monroe	April 28	5
Otto von Bismarck	April 1	5
Gladstone	December 29	5
Abraham Lincoln	February 12	5
Voltaire	November 21	5
Dean Swift	November 30	5
Cardinal Newman	February 21	5
Mark Twain	November 30	5
Winston Churchill	November 30	5
Faraday	October 22	5
Lord Byron	January 22	5
Schubert	January 31	5
Sir Isaac Pitman	January 4	5

Name	Birthdate	Vedic Birth Code#
Sir Francis Bacon	January 22	5
Cardinal Richelieu	September 5	5
Napoleon I	August 15	5
Lord Alfred Tennyson	August 6	5
Lord Balfour	July 25	5
John Wesley	June 17	5
Bruce Jenner	June 17	5
Prince Albert/Monaco	August 26	5
Nicholas II of Russia	May 18	5
Sir James Barrie	May 9	5
Duke of Wellington	May 1	6
Napoleon III	April 20	6
George Pullman	March 3	6
Rudyard Kipling	December 30	6
Lord Baden Powell	February 22	6
George Elliot	November 22	6
George Washington	February 22	6
Subhas Bose	January 23	6
John D. Rockefeller	July 8	6
La Fontaine	July 8	6
George Bernard Shaw	July 26	6
George Stephenson	June 9	6
Brigham Young	June 1	7
Thomas Carlyle	December 4	7
Hinrieh Heine	December 13	7
Jawaharlal Nehru	November 14	7
Samuel Pepys	February 23	7
Tallyrand	February 14	7
Joan of Arc	January 6	7
Frederick the Great	January 24	7
George Westinghouse	October 6	7
Bonar Law	September 16	7
Louis XIV	September 16	7
Queen Elizabeth	September 7	7

Name	Birthdate	Vedic Birth Code#
Alexander the Great	July 1	8
Alexandre Dumas	July 28	8
Orville Wright	August 19	8
Thomas Hardy	June 2	8
Immanuel Kant	April 22	8
Sir Henry Irving	February 6	8
John Knox	November 24	8
Oscar Wilde	October 16	8
Richard I Lion-Hearted	September 8	8
Herbert Hoover	August 10	9
King George V	June 3	9
Sir Arthur Conan Doyle	May 22	9
Thomas Huxley	May 4	9
William Shakespeare	April 23	9
Elizabeth Browning	March 6	9
Michelangelo	March 6	9
Sir Walter Scott	December 6	9
Max Muller	December 6	9
King George	December 24	9
Warren Hastings	December 6	9
Andrew Carnegie	November 25	9
Wilkie Collins	January 8	9
David Lloyd George	January 17	9

Appendix 3

Birthdates & Vedic Birth Codes of Famous People & Major Events

Famous Name	Date	Vedic Code
Muhammed Ali	01/18/1942	1
Warren Beatty	03/30/1937	6
Marlon Brando	04/03/1924	7
Tom Brokaw	02/06/1940	8
Charles Bronson	11/03/1922	5
Carol Burnett	04/26/1933	3
Johnny Carson	10/23/1925	6
Jimmy Carter	10/14/1924	6
Fidel Castro	08/13/1926	3
Prince Charles	11/14/1948	7
Cher	05/20/1946	7
Dick Clark	03/30/1945	6
Bill Clinton	08/19/1946	9
Hillary Clinton	10/16/1947	9
Bill Cosby	07/12/1937	1
Ted Danson	12/29/1947	5
Robert DeNiro	08/17/1943	7
Phil Donahue	12/21/1935	6
Michael Douglas	09/25/1944	7
Clint Eastwood	05/31/1930	9
Jane Fonda	12/21/1937	6
Gerald Ford	07/14/1913	3
Harrison Ford	07/04/1942	2
Al Gore	03/31/1948	7
Tipper Gore	08/19/1948	9
Goldie Hawn	11/21/1945	5
Hugh Hefner	04/09/1926	4
DustinHoffman	08/08/1937	7
Bob Hope	05/29/1903	7
Michael Jackson	08/28/1958	9

Famous Name	Date	Vedic Code
Jesse Jackson	10/08/1941	9
Ann Jillian	01/29/1950	3
Pope John Paul II	05/18/1920	5
Jerry Lewis	05/16/1926	3
Andrea Macko	10/28/1966	2
Kamini Maragh	04/12/1968	7
Ramesh Maragh	01/30/1964	4
Dean Martin	06/17/1917	5
Paul McCartney	06/18/1942	6
Paul Newman	01/26/1925	9
Jack Nicholson	04/22/1937	8
Richard Nixon	01/08/1913	1
Al Pacino	04/25/1940	2
Dolly Parton	01/19/1946	2
Elvis Presley	01/08/1935	9
Richard Pryor	12/01/1940	4
Nancy Reagan	07/06/1923	4
Ronald Reagan	02/06/1911	8
Robert Redford	08/18/1937	8
Burt Reynolds	02/11/1936	4
Diana Ross	03/26/1944	2
Brooke Shields	05/31/1965	9
Frank Sinatra	12/12/1917	6
Steven Spielberg	12/18/1947	3
Bruce Springsteen	09/23/1949	5
Sly Stallone	07/06/1946	4
James Stewart	05/20/1908	7
Meryl Streep	06/22/1949	1
Barbra Streisand	04/24/1942	1
Elizabeth Taylor	02/27/1932	2
John Travolta	02/18/1954	2
Barbara Walters	09/25/1931	7
Stevie Wonder	05/13/1950	9
Tammy Wynette	05/05/1942	1
Jeffrey Dahmer	05/21/1966	8
Jerry Rubin	07/14/1938	3

Famous Name	Date	Vedic Code
Empress Nagako	03/06/1905	9
Alex Trebek's daughter	08/16/1993	6
Stewart Granger	05/06/1913	2
Alan Dershowitz	09/01/1938	1
Christie Brinkley's son	06/02/1995	8
Elizabeth Montgomery	04/15/1933	1
Angier Biddle Duke	11/20/1915	4
Erich Leinsdorf	02/04/1912	6
Nancy Kerrigan	10/13/1970	5
Jorge Luis Borges	08/24/1899	5
Frederico Fellini	01/20/1920	3
Cesar Romero	02/15/1907	8
Norman Vincent Peale	05/31/1898	9
Robert Cecil Williams	01/10/1909	2
Bill Bixby	01/22/1934	5
David Koresh	09/15/1959	6
Joey Buttafucco	03/11/1956	5
Darzen Petrovic	10/22/1964	5
Kathie Lee Gifford	08/16/1953	6
Vita Sackville-West	03/09/1892	3
Rush Limbaugh	01/12/1951	4
Mikhail Gorbachev	03/02/1931	5
Prince Takahito Mikasa	12/02/1915	5
Shu Kawashima	07/26/1973	6
Misugu Akimoto	06/01/1955	7
Takuma Miyamoto	01/09/1993	1
Danny DeVito	11/17/1944	1
Magic Johnson	06/04/1992	1
Brennan Karem	06/26/1992	5
Tiffany Trump	10/13/1993	5
Montel Williams II	09/17/1993	8
Vesna Vulovic	08/06/1949	5
Slobodan Milosevic	08/20/1940	1
Mickey Mouse	11/18/1928	2
Michael Caine	03/14/1933	8
Frank Sinatra	12/12/1915	6

Famous Name	Date	Vedic Code
Dodi al Fayed	04/15/1955	1
Gianni Versace	12/02/1946	5
Drew Carey	05/23/1958	1
Luis Donaldo Colosio	02/10/1950	3
Arsenio Hall	02/12/1956	5
Augustine Ann Brooks	05/03/1994	8

Event	Date	Vedic Code
Birth on the highway	07/14/1938	3
Dangerous fire	08/08/1994	7
Kitchen fire	08/07/1994	6
House fire	12/21/1994	6
House fire	12/20/1994	5
House fire	12/17/1994	5
Cruise ship inferno	11/30/1994	5
Explosion/NY subway	12/21/1994	6
Baby born on freeway	02/03/1995	5
Dead back to life	10/29/1993	3
Norway tankers collide	02/05/1995	7
Chinese rocket blows	01/26/195	9
Car bomb kills dozens	01/30/1995	4
Truck kills 7 at school	08/13/1993	3
Ca traffic pile-up	11/29/1991	4
Chris Reeves accident	05/27/1995	5
Hidden gun law/TX	05/26/1995	4
Earthquake in Russia	05/28/1995	6
Deadly subway crash	06/05/1995	2
Car bomb in Peru	05/24/1994	2
Dispatcher aids birth	01/08/1994	9
LA earthquake	01/17/1994	9
Killer tornado, OK	04/24/1993	1
Argentina tornado	05/06/1992	2
Argentina tornado	11/25/1985	9
Volcano eruption	10/18/1992	1
Monica Seles stabbing	04/30/1993	7
Royal wedding, Japan	06/09/1993	6

Event	Date	Vedic Code
Restore hope	12/09/1992	3
Clinton's mother dies	11/19/1992	3
Windsor Castle fire	11/20/1992	4
Reba McEntire crash	11/06/1992	8
Oil tanker crash, Spain	12/03/1992	6
Baby left in -0°	02/02/1993	4
Birth in custody	01/18/1993	1
Baby born on subway	01/11/1993	3
Abandoned baby	01/06/1993	7
Israel-Palestine Accord	09/13/1993	4
Chicago storm	07/02/1992	9
CA Angels bus crash	05/21/1992	8
Tragic car crash	06/02/1992	8
Addict kills parents	03/26/1970	2
Irish cease fire	08/31/1994	3
USAir crash	09/08/1994	8
Penn Station blaze	09/11/1994	2
Oklahoma City blast	04/19/1999	5
Fatal tornado	03/27/1956	3
Killer bee attack	11/03/1994	5

CPSIA information can be obtained at www.ICGtesting.com
Printed in the USA
BVOW020845281212

309136BV00002B/179/A